SOARING
My Improbable Life

Major Alphonso B. Jones
Co-authored by Kim Nelson

BookLocker
Saint Petersburg, Florida

Print ISBN: 978-1-64719-347-8
Epub ISBN: 978-1-64719-348-5
Mobi ISBN: 978-1-64719-349-2

Published by BookLocker.com, Inc., St. Petersburg, Florida.

Printed on acid-free paper.

BookLocker.com, Inc.
2021

First Edition

Library of Congress Cataloguing in Publication Data
Jones, Major Alphonso B.; Nelson, Kim
SOARING: My Improbable Life by Major Alphonso B. Jones,
co-authored by Kim Nelson
Library of Congress Control Number: 2021901218

To my grandchildren—may you walk in faith and always follow your dreams.

Contents

FOREWARD

I have often pondered why my father, who has lived an extraordinary life, was able to accomplish so much having grown up poor and black during the Great Depression. In the unlikeliest of eras, he had the audacity to dream big and his sense of his own possibilities was seemingly limitless. What gave him the confidence and resilience to navigate a world that was so hostile to him then, just as it is to so many young black men today? Was it his loving family or the teachers and mentors he met along the way? Was it his deep Catholic faith or just his innate optimism? I ponder these questions not only to understand my father's achievements against the odds but also because their implications are clear: if he did it, others can too.

When my dad first told me that he had finally decided to put his story to paper, I rejoiced because I knew it would be a priceless gift to our family (present and future). As I actually began to read the manuscript, I saw that its importance extended beyond the confines of our own family. Dad's story is a part of a much bigger story: that of black achievement in America, against all odds.

Dad was born in a nation and capital city where segregation and racism were woven into the fabric of the law and society, and yet he succeeded in getting an education; achieving his dream of flying; seeing the world; finding the love of his life; fighting in a war for a country that barely accepted him; raising three happy, successful children; teaching countless young people and adults; and spending his life making the world a better place. Dad somehow avoided the alcohol, drugs, and prison that often engulf the lives of black men, robbing them of their dreams, beating them into submission, and leaving them feeling enraged, in despair, and trapped in a world that doesn't seem to have a place for them. Dad's story offers an important model for young black men struggling to navigate their own journeys. He has worked hard, no question, but he has also experienced great joy and has approached each day with a happy heart and positive attitude.

Surely there is a lesson for all of us in my father's life. What does it mean to believe in yourself? To seize opportunities as they come your way? To live right? What happens if you put faith in the center of your life and give and receive love freely? What if you always seek to improve each community you become a part of? What if you approach every day with a sense of possibility and joy?

If I seem a little effusive in my praise, I will admit I've always been a Daddy's girl. I have heard many of the stories in this book a hundred times, some while sitting on my father's knee as a child. And I am a *part* of my father's story. So much of him resides in me. Every triumph I can claim can be traced back to the lessons I learned and the love I received from him. I have only gradually understood the gift of growing up with such a man. Being raised by someone who doesn't worry about what *can't* be done but just focuses on what *should* be done has subconsciously influenced my own choices and decisions.

My father is now eighty-nine years old and deeply content with the life he has created. He spends his time volunteering at his church, where, pre-Covid-19, he attended daily Mass each morning, engaged in family events, and traveled the world. In 2019 alone, Mom and Dad traveled to Paris, New York, Las Vegas, Denver, Hawaii, Minneapolis, Texas, and San Diego. They journeyed to see grandchildren's performances, to welcome a new family member into the world, for birthdays, graduations, retirements, holidays, and family reunions—wherever the party was. They are living large and squeezing every last drop out of these golden years they have been granted.

And while my father is slowing down a bit, and his mobility is increasingly limited, his spirit of adventure, his faith, his commitment to family, and his sense of humor have not changed at all. He still loves nothing more than a good game of bid whist, preferably one he is winning, and is always ready for that next adventure around the corner. I have always wanted to grow up to be just like my father; perhaps, after hearing his incredible story, others will too.

Kim Nelson,
Co-author

PREFACE

After reading Gail Buckley's book on the life of her mother, Lena Horne, I decided to jot down a few words about my own life. Lena Horne and I actually have something of a personal connection as I met her at a Broadway show that my daughter, Leilani Jones Wilmore, starred in. Lena was fifteen years older than me, so her story was in the same general timeframe as mine.

In her book, Gail mentions that in order for a black person to achieve his American dream, he has to be stronger, faster, and smarter than most. I had come to this conclusion too!

Gail talks about sifting through a trunkful of saved photographs, documents, souvenirs, letters, receipts, and newspaper clippings. She said that what you have saved helps you remember where you have been. I, too, started looking through boxes where I had stored pieces of my past and began getting everything into some kind of order. I suddenly decided to write it all down. I knew I could do it. This was the start of a book of my life.

I am grateful to all of those who have helped me piece the story of my life together. My wife, Muriel, has been so helpful in recounting dates, places, and experiences I have long forgotten. After all, in many ways, this is the story of her life too. My children and extended family have also been helpful in reminding me of stories they remember and are a part of. Recreating my life's history has been an enormous undertaking, and I want to thank my family for their help and support on this journey. I especially want to thank my daughter Kim, who helped me organize my thoughts and write a book worthy of publishing. Kim tackled this challenge with love, patience, enthusiasm, skill, and tenacity. Lastly, I want to thank my daughter, Angie, and my granddaughter, Sammie, who read and provided detailed notes on the manuscript.

I wrote this book for my children and grandchildren so that they will remember the great times we have shared over the years and know how much they have always been loved. I also wrote this book for Muriel and me so that we will always have a way to remember our beautiful life together. And at some point, in the future, when I start to think *I couldn't possibly have done all of this*, I can look through my military orders, certificates, and other papers I assembled to write the book, to validate the written word and remind me that it all really did happen.

HUMBLE BEGINNINGS

I was born on January 25, 1932, in the midst of the Great Depression. My father, Beverly Jones, was the son of a Baptist minister from Virginia. He was a tall, handsome man with a good job and a car. He had an athletic build, brown eyes, and a mustache. He had a pleasant voice, winning smile, and sense of humor that instantly put you at ease. He didn't talk much, but when he did, you felt it was worthwhile to listen.

My father worked as an automobile mechanic in a garage, fixing the cars of wealthy owners, so his job was not affected much by the Depression. He'd sometimes earn extra money as a taxi driver in his spare time. He was always busy working. My father always seemed to be preparing my brother and me for a life of hardship for black boys living in a white man's world. We grew up understanding that we were expected to work hard, pray, have a good sense of humor, and do our best at all times. And even if life sometimes seemed too hard to bear, we were to never give up but to persevere and continue to do our very best. We understood these lessons later in life, but at that time we didn't have a clue what he was talking about. My twin brother and I loved him very much and tried to measure up as best we could.

My mother was a very special woman. The daughter of a Catholic family from Maryland, she was short and slim, with long black hair and beautiful brown eyes. Her voice was soft and loving. We knew she believed we were special by her attitude toward us. She always made excuses to my father for my curious nature. My father would say,

"Honey, what's wrong with that boy?" whenever I did something he didn't approve of, like taking the clock apart to see how it worked.

"There is nothing wrong with him," she would say with a smile. "He is just curious." She solved the problem by getting old clocks from the thrift store for me to tinker with.

Mother was always neat and tidy and made sure we were too. She prayed a lot and taught us to kneel before her and say our prayers daily. My brother and I were the recipients of multiple hugs and kisses daily. Her love surrounded us all the days of our lives.

My parents met and fell in love in Washington, DC, in 1931. They were not accepted by either family because of differences in religion, but also because my father was from Virginia and my mother was from Maryland. In those days, folks from Maryland and Virginia did not mix and Baptists did not marry Catholics. Catholics had to get special permission to marry someone outside of the faith. Permission would be granted if it was agreed that the children would be raised in the Catholic faith. My father agreed, so the Catholic Church sanctioned the marriage, which finally earned the acceptance of Mother's relatives. They were married by a Catholic priest. Later in life, my father converted to Catholicism.

Dad was "Mr. Fix It." The parishioners would ask for help, and he would fix whatever needed fixing with a smile, even if they couldn't pay. Mother took in kids after school and watched them until their parents could pick them up after work. I remember the cakes and cookies she made for the church; there were always plenty left for us. Much later, when my mother died, the director of the funeral home told me of the fond memories he had waiting for his parents to pick him up at Mother's house when he was a child.

My mother became pregnant with twins, which she had prayed for, thinking it would unite the families. In answer to her prayers, on January 25, 1932, my brother and I were born—identical twins. To make life interesting, she named us both Al! My birth name is Alphonsus Beverly Jones, and my twin brother's name is Aloysius Fredroy Jones, but we both went by Al.

When we were younger, it was nearly impossible to tell us apart, though I was born with a small extra finger on my left hand next to my little finger. Old-timers said this was a special blessing and a sign of good luck. They were right because when I was older, the girls loved to touch my extra finger. They would go crazy with excitement! Later, in the Air Force, they had to cut my extra finger off because it got in the way.

My mother and father's families could not resist coming to see the identical twins, and in this way, the two families were indeed united.

When we would visit my grandfather, the Reverend Beverly F. Jones Sr., during his church revivals once a year, he always had my brother and me stay with him. The rest of the family stayed with other relatives. We knew he loved us, and we were as glad to be with him as he was to see us. Later, as teens, we enjoyed discussing matters of faith with our grandfather. Those visits with him remain some of my fondest memories.

Washington was a great city to grow up in. Many African Americans were able to get in the many government and business offices. My father got a job in the Government Printing Office. My Uncle Tommy, who worked there first, sponsored him.

In DC, the history of our country was laid out before us in the many museums of the Smithsonian. I visited these museums as well as many other historic sites when I was young, but I still wanted to see the world.

I still remember my first day of school. My brother and I were excited to be going and couldn't understand why our mother was crying. The school was a single-story building made of red bricks with a lawn in the front yard, located a few blocks from our home. My mother left us in the classroom and went home.

Our teacher was a bespectacled black woman with the stern air of a disciplinarian. When she saw my brother and me talking to one another, she shouted, "No talking!" That was the first time someone had ever yelled at us like that.

When she was not looking, we ran back home. We knocked on our front door, and our mother swept us up in her arms with kisses. She gave us cookies and milk and waited for us to tell her what went wrong. We told her how the teacher shouted at us! Mother took us back to school the next morning and told the teacher not to shout at her boys. She said, "Just separate them, and everything will be fine." The teacher soon found that we were good students, among the best in the class.

Outside of class, my brother and I were inseparable! We went everywhere together, did everything together, and seemed to agree on just about everything. I know it's hard to believe, but we seldom argued or fought. We were incredibly close and loved exchanging thoughts and ideas with one another. It was as if we were two halves of the same person. In all of our conversations, each person's aim was to meet the other halfway. Whenever we reached a spot where we could not agree, we dropped the topic and never talked about it again. We were entirely sympathetic to each other as twins.

Our family was growing rapidly. After Al and I were born, my sister Beulah came a year later. There was a break of a few years, and then sister Fredia, brother Robert, and another sister, Doris, were all born.

Both of my parents worked extremely hard to earn enough money to pay all the bills and take care of us. My mother worked from 4 p.m. to midnight cleaning Amtrak passenger trains, and my father worked from 11 p.m. to 7 a.m. Mother said, "You three kids need to learn how to help take care of the house and each other" and Beulah, Aloysius, and I were expected to chip in on household chores like shopping, cooking, cleaning, laundry, and the dishes to help our household run smoothly. My brother and I got jobs delivering newspapers before school to help out. As I was the oldest child, I was in charge, followed by my twin brother and my sister, who was a year younger than him.

We loved our parents very much and were eager to please them. They were happy together and with us. I cannot ever remember my mother getting really angry with us. If we had to be disciplined, she would do it, but it was rarely necessary.

One evening, I let my mother down. When she came home from work, the dishes were not done. She washed them and put them away before going to bed. The next morning, I cried when I saw the kitchen clean. She never mentioned it, but I promised myself I would try not to let her down again. I knew that she had to depend on us to do our part. The life skills I learned as a child would carry well into my adult life and even my marriage. I grew up understanding that everyone needs to share responsibility for housework when both parents are working and only later realized that this belief was not universally held by my male peers.

Mother took us to church to be altar boys when we were eleven years old. Holy Redeemer Catholic Church was a large building with a big staircase leading up to the entrance. Beautiful organ music played during Mass and six large lighted candles graced the altar.

The church custodian, Ishmael, taught us all that we would need to know in order to serve as altar boys at Mass. Ishmael looked like he was from Egypt. He was of medium height with wavy black hair and a calm and pleasant voice. He was extremely knowledgeable about the Catholic Church, and Mother knew we were in good hands with him. He liked us, and we liked him.

Father Kelly, our pastor, was a tall, slightly overweight man with a ruddy face, white hair, and a twinkle in his eye. He spoke with an Irish accent, which we thought was funny. He seemed wealthy to our young eyes, but had mastered the art of helping others in a way that did not hurt their dignity. He was the first white person we really spent time with, and we liked him very much. We helped Father Kelly at the daily 8 a.m. Mass before school. We liked weddings and funerals best of all because we were excused from school for a few hours and always got a tip from the family after the service.

Father Kelly knew that most of the parents couldn't afford the special black shoes that were required at Mass, so one day he took all his altar boys to the shoe store and bought us each a pair (plus ice cream and lunch afterward). I will never forget Father Kelly's kindness toward us. Mass was in Latin, which we studied in the sixth grade. The kids in our school thought we were rich. We had new shoes; black, fur-collar leather coats; and money in our pockets. We didn't tell them the shoes had been given to us at church and the expensive-looking coats were "hand-me-downs" from our aunt, who worked for a rich family who had twins. Our newspaper route allowed us a little extra pocket change and we felt very rich indeed.

We lived most of our lives one block from our church, together in a big house with the families of some of my mother's sisters to share expenses. It was a three-story, walk-up row house in a working-class neighborhood. It was home to us and always filled with the noise of kids running around and the wonderful aroma of home-cooking. It smelled like home. We grew up very close to our cousins, even when we moved a few blocks away to our own home years later.

Our household was full of love and laughter—and lots of boys. Sometimes, my mother's brother, Uncle Richard, would babysit us.

Uncle Richard was tall and medium-built. He was a pleasant person who loved all of us, and everyone loved him. Once a day, he would line up the boys and give each of us a whack on our behinds.

I said, "What's that for?! We haven't done anything wrong!"

"That's just in case you do!" he answered.

Once, when we boys had grown to be teens, we visited Uncle Richard on his birthday. We planned the visit carefully. We invited Uncle Richard to come out to the backyard to receive his gifts from all of us boys. We sang "Happy Birthday," but as we ended the song, we all grabbed him at once! We didn't hurt him, but he couldn't move. We told him our first gift for him was a few whacks to pay him back for the whacks we received when we were younger. We really did have gifts, but we were going to give him the whacks first. After Uncle Richard got his whacks, he started to laugh and said we got him good.

As children, we loved to go riding in our father's car, especially to the zoo or to the airport. The car was black with soft seats. With the windows down, the air smelled clean and breezy. I couldn't understand how my father could make the car go and stop by pressing the correct pedal on the floor without looking. It was magic.

On those outings, we would typically pack a picnic and enjoyed sitting under a tree in the shade having our lunch, then walking around the zoo to see all the different animals we read about in books. At the airport, we would watch the people getting on and off the planes. In those days, people dressed up when they traveled. I knew they came from or were returning to all of the wonderful places I read about in books. I dreamed of traveling around the world one day and visiting those places too.

During summer and winter school breaks, my twin and I lived on our Aunt Pearl and Uncle Clem Dyson's tobacco farm in Bushwood, Maryland, to keep us away from street gangs in Washington and, I suspect, to offset the cost of feeding two growing boys. We loved it! Aunt Pearl was tall and thin with a kind voice and a loving personality. She always made everyone feel at home around her and was an attentive listener who treated us like her own children. Aunt Pearl took my mother into her home when my mother was young, and my mother often shared stories of living with her sister Pearl. Uncle Clem had an aura of health and industry about him that came from working hard on a farm all of one's life.

Uncle Clem welcomed my brother and me staying with them because we were strong, hard workers—city boys who saw farm work as new and exciting. He also saw us as companions for his son, Richard, who was around our age.

Richard was a little shorter than us and was smart and tricky. One day, we asked if we could help with the farm work. He said he didn't know if we could do it right since we were city boys. He was so sneaky! We said we would each give him a dime if he let us help. Imagine— paying him to do his work! How dumb can you get? But the truth was his chores were fun for us city boys. There were other benefits too: Aunt Pearl and Uncle Clem allowed us to glean vegetables from their farm. It was fun picking berries because we could eat as many as we wanted while we picked.

The farmhouse was spacious, with a big wood oven used for cooking meals and, in winter months, it provided heat for the whole house. Aunt Pearl had a frying pan with a cover on it, suspended over the fire on a long pole. When we visited in the winter, she put hot charcoals in the pan and stuck the pan under the covers until the bed was toasty and warm. My brother and I would jump in the warm bed and pull up the covers to stay warm until morning.

We cut wood for the stove that provided heat and a place for cooking because there was no gas. We drew water from the well for drinking, cooking, and taking weekly baths because there wasn't running water in the house. The toilet was outside the house. At night, we only had an oil lamp to see by. The people in the country did not have electricity. Visiting the tobacco farm made us appreciate all the modern conveniences we enjoyed at our home in Washington, DC.

Just because we lived in the city didn't mean we didn't know how to make the most of what we had. My mother was so clever. She made her own wine for our family and canned food in the summer to be eaten in the winter. Mother went to a community cannery that had all the supplies for canning (which always seemed an odd choice of words to me because actually they used jars). Mother would put so much food in jars. It lasted quite a while. One summer, there were explosions in the pantry. The heat was causing some of the jars to explode! What a mess!

My mother gave us the responsibility of looking out for our sister Beulah. Beulah was so beautiful that we knew it would not be easy. Beulah was a petite girl with a very fair complexion; long, wavy brown hair; and striking green eyes. She was a headstrong young lady and had a voice that could shatter glass if she was angry with you! Beulah always stood out in a crowd of students because of her unique appearance, her confidence, and her natural intelligence. She was smarter than me, but I made up for it by working harder. We never told Beulah that our mother had told us to look after her. We would have protected her anyway because we loved our baby sister so much. Growing up, Beulah and I were as close as a brother and sister could be.

One day, we had to fight a big high school football player who had been annoying Beulah. He was a big kid, definitely someone you did not want to mess with. We were small and light, but we were fast. We went outside after school and danced around him, taking turns hitting him and then dancing out of his way. His heavier weight worked against him. He slowed down quickly, while we could dance around him all day.

When he was exhausted, we told him we were willing to stop and shake hands and that we actually didn't want to fight but we had to protect our sister. So, he offered to call it even, and we stopped fighting and became friends.

A BIG DREAM

The world was at war in the '40s. Every movie theater showed newsreel updates of the war. President Roosevelt's fireside chats had a calming effect and gave us the feeling that everything was going to be okay, but it was a time of great uncertainty. It was during this time that I began to think about my own possibilities.

In 1943, when I was eleven years old and in the sixth grade, I decided I wanted to travel and see the world when I grew up. I had read books about different countries and wanted to visit them. I especially wanted to see the Holy Land and experience the places where Jesus walked. I had read about places where people said Jesus' mother appeared to someone with a message about the future. Maybe I could find a job that would allow me to travel.

I was so excited by this dream that I told my science teacher, Mr. Jackson, a slim, smart-looking man, about it and asked him if he thought it would be possible for me to find a job that would allow me to travel the world.

Mr. Jackson said, "Boy, you better get yourself a good mop and a good broom so you can become a good janitor." I was devastated. It was as if he had taken a pin to the big balloon of my dream and all of my hopes slowly began to seep out.

Later that day, I asked my English teacher, Mrs. Catlett, if she thought I could ever find a job that would allow me to travel the world. Mrs. Catlett had a medium build and a nice voice that made you feel that she loved and cared about you. You somehow knew she would always be there to help you.

"Of course, you do!" she exclaimed. "Let me do some research to give you some ideas."

She came back to me with a list of books to read and told me it would require hard work, but my dream was achievable. She had contacted an Air Force recruiter, who said that if I could graduate high school with a grade point average of 3.0 or higher and complete at least one year of college, I could enter the Air Force and take a test to enter the Officer Flight Training School.

Mrs. Catlett put the thought in my head that a career in the US Air Force would allow me to see the world. Her aspiration was not just for me to join the Air Force but for me to become an officer. What could have possessed her to think such a thing could be possible for a poor, black boy in 1943?

"Is this a path you want to pursue, Alphonso?" Mrs. Catlett asked. The question buzzed around in my head all day long and throughout the weeks that followed.

I talked it over with my twin brother, and he was interested too. Neither of us could have imagined how Mrs. Catlett's idea would take up residence in our minds and provide us with motivation, focus, and purpose in the coming years.

Mrs. Catlett kept providing us with books to read and even passed the reading list to our seventh-grade teacher. I later realized she had inspired me to be a teacher when I eventually left the Air Force. I've never forgotten the power of one committed, positive adult to change a child's life forever. I came back to visit Mrs. Catlett over the years to update her on my career and thank her again and again for believing in me and helping me see a future I could not have imagined on my own.

Now, my brother and I had a powerful dream and clarity on how to achieve it. But how were we going to pay for college?

"There are options," Mrs. Catlett told us. "You have two ways: through a sports scholarship or through an academic scholarship."

This had implications for our choice of high school. When it came time to select ours, we had a couple of choices. The closest high school to our home was Dunbar, which had a reputation for excelling at preparing black students for higher education, but my brother and I had different plans. We were inspired by Jesse Owens winning four gold medals in the 1936 Olympics and became fixated on the idea of becoming track athletes and going to college on an athletic scholarship. This was not an unreasonable goal; we were both thin as rails and had always been fast. We had heard that Cardozo High School had the best track coach in Washington, DC—Sal Hall. Coach Hall had a proven record of training black boys to become champions.

We talked it over with our parents, and learned they didn't really want us to go to Cardozo; after all, we lived a couple of blocks from the best college prep school for black kids in Washington. First, we had to convince our parents to allow us to go to Cardozo High School, then we had to convince Coach Hall that we had what it took and to get a district exception to attend his school.

We called Coach Hall and asked if we could come and visit him. My brother and I walked the thirty minutes to the school from our home, brimming with all the confidence that fifteen-year-old boys could muster. Coach Hall was our ticket to college, and we could not fail. Coach Hall's office was small and cramped, but what captured our attention at once was the case of trophies along one wall. We opened the conversation, saying directly, "Coach Hall, we want to become champions!" Coach Hall had an athletic build, the ability to size you up in one glance, and a no-nonsense voice that was used to giving orders that were obeyed instantly. He looked down at the two scrawny twins before him with skepticism. We hardly looked like championship material.

"Are you willing to work hard, as hard as necessary, to become champions?" he asked in his customary no-nonsense tone.

Somehow, when we both enthusiastically shouted "Yes!" he saw our determination. He sat up in his chair and decided, "Well, I can make you champions!" He got us assigned to Cardozo.

Coach Hall worked our butts off. He had us run a golf course in boots to build our leg and lung capacity. If one of us complained, "Coach, my legs are sore," he would shoot back, "Get your parents to rub your legs down—keep those boots on!"

Or if we said, "Coach, my side is hurting," he'd respond with: "Good. That means your body is developing. Run through the pain. You can't be a champion if you don't run through the pain. I'm going to tell you the secret between a champion and a wannabe. A champion runs through the pain, and the wannabe just can't."

Coach Hall understood that becoming a champion had nothing to do with size; it had everything to do with determination, growth, and ability. And sure enough, in time, the pain disappeared as our bodies grew stronger and faster.

We also joined the High School Cadet Corps our first two years of high school. We learned about the military and wore magnificent uniforms with sabers. We joined the United States Navy Reserves our last two years in high school. We only had to meet one Saturday a month and two weeks a year training on Naval aircraft carrier CV-42, called the *FDR*.

Between training and studying for our classes, we didn't have much time for other things, but I enjoyed high school very much. We were very popular. The girls would hang around us and always wanted to feel my extra little finger. They got so excited that I started putting my left hand in my pocket when they were around.

By the time I graduated, I had won the national high school indoor mile championship at the Penn Relays and was one of the best high school milers in America. My brother and three others had set the world record for the high school mile relay. We spent most of our time studying and running track. We traveled to track meets up and down the East Coast, competing and winning. Because we were identical twins and both went by Al Jones, we were sometimes mistaken for being the same person.

Spectators and other coaches would criticize Coach Hall for overworking "the poor track star," as we ran and won both sprint and distance races. He finally had to show us together to make it clear that we were two different people.

We graduated from Cardozo in June 1950 with high honors. In the end, the grueling effort and constant hard work paid off: Between my brother and me, we were offered scholarships to seventeen colleges: three scholastic and fourteen athletic for track. Learning that if I worked hard, I could achieve my goals was a lesson I would apply again and again throughout my life.

A NEW WORLD

The University of Michigan paid for us to visit the summer before graduation and granted both my brother and me full scholarships, all expenses paid. Michigan wanted us and was willing to go the extra mile to get us. We were sold! We entered the University of Michigan in the fall of 1950.

That year, Michigan had one of the top milers in America (me) and one of the top milers from Canada, a guy named George. George appeared to be everything I was not. He was white, tall, and a skilled pacemaker who had style and conviction that he could beat me with no trouble at all. I, however, had developed my body into a running machine that could keep up with anyone and then draw on reserve power to turn on a burst of energy at the end of the race. I barreled past the finish line so fast in some races that I had to slow down in stages.

There were a lot of bets placed on who would win the first race in which we both ran. My style of running was to lay back in the race and sprint during the last lap. I studied George's style. He was a great runner who could pace himself all the way to the finish line. George was used to being out in front and staying there to the finish. I knew that if I stayed behind him, he would be at ease during our race.

The big day came, and I stayed back until the gun was fired for the last lap. I ran past him like he was running backward and finished way ahead of him! After I won the race, I ran my customary extra lap to cool down, and someone handed me a school flag to wave. The fans stood up and cheered as I passed by! Could life get any better than that for a college athlete?

Michigan was a new world for me. Washington was segregated most of my life, and I had grown up in a largely all-black world. Michigan was the first school I attended that was integrated. It was a whole new world for my brother and I in other ways, as well. For the first time, my brother and I went to concerts, plays, and football games. Michigan had a football and track stadium that seated one hundred thousand people! When I attended football games in the late fall, I would boil eggs and wrap them in my pockets to provide additional warmth. When they cooled down, I ate them while drinking hot chocolate.

When we first arrived in Michigan, we were assigned to Fletcher Hall, a dormitory for freshman athletes. During the first few months, we had to study at certain times, and they had professors on each floor to help us if we needed it.

My favorite course was Air Science. Dr. Losh, my professor, was one of the best—so they told me. She was tall and wore dark-rimmed glasses. She was an expert in our galaxy, the stars, and outer space. I learned a lot about space, the stars and planets, and constellations. I got an A in that class. Dr. Losh helped me form a strong foundational understanding of the universe I would draw on later in my professional career.

One day, my brother and I were in the park at night studying the sky when the police confronted us. They thought we were up to no good at that time of night and arrested us. I called the track coach, who then called the police chief, who then told his officers to drive us back to the school.

There were advantages to being successful student athletes at Michigan. My brother and I were known throughout the small college town of Ann Arbor. We had a car on campus and would load it up with our athlete friends. When we needed gas, we would give the gas station attendant whatever cash we had between us, and they would always fill it up to help us out. This was one of the ways the folks in town showed how proud they were of all of us.

I joined the Pershing Rifles Corps at Michigan, a military-type unit in uniform. We met once a month and studied Army matters. I was still in the Navy Reserve, but there was no conflict between the two because I only got paid for attending Navy Reserve classes two weeks a year in the summer.

My brother and I joined the Alpha Phi Alpha fraternity in our sophomore year and moved into their spacious house on campus. Alpha Phi Alpha was an African American fraternity, and it was great to belong to a group of accomplished, young, African American men. My brother ended up being the "House Mother" who helped set rules in accordance with those of the school. We enjoyed great parties at the house and had a lot of fun, particularly with the ladies.

Whenever a new girl came to one of our parties, we would all wait for her to go to the restroom. In the restroom, there was a large picture of a naked man on the wall with a flap over his private parts. Unbeknownst to the young co-eds, the flap was wired to a bell, so, when they lifted the flap, the bell would ring, and everyone would cheer. They *always* peeked under the flap!

Sometimes we would put a tape recorder under the couch, turn it on, and then leave the girls alone. Later, we would play it back to hear who they were talking about when they were left alone. We were a sneaky bunch!

My brother and I worked as hard as we could and won most of our races at Michigan. Despite the full ride at Michigan and the part-time jobs my brother and I took on, money was tight. My goal was still to join the Air Force as soon as I had successfully completed the required number of college credits, as Mrs. Catlett and I had discussed when I was in sixth grade. Once I had the credits I needed, I would be ready to move on.

One day I sat down with my brother and said, "It's time for me to go. I've completed all of the requirements to get into the Aviation Cadet Program, and I am going to leave Michigan now to enlist." Aloysius replied, "I am not sure what I want to do with my life yet, but I know I want to graduate from Michigan. If I stay, I'll have a couple more years to figure out what's right for me."

I was torn by my brother's decision to stay at the University of Michigan until he graduated, but I knew it was time for me to go. I would get my college degree later. We hugged and said goodbye. I told my brother I would send him money as soon as I became an officer. Leaving Aloysius, who had been by my side my entire life, was much harder than I expected. I was truly on my own, and for the first time, I was lonely. I knew I was making the right choice for me. My dreams were calling.

AN OFFICER AND A GENTLEMAN

I had been a member of the Navy Reserve since high school, and in 1952, upon leaving Michigan, I applied to take the test for admission to the Navy's flight program. I felt I was well-positioned to be considered for the program because I had three and a half years in the Naval Reserve (while in high school and college), and I had completed all of the requirements at a top-notch academic institution, but I was not accepted into the program. The Navy did not want me. I felt betrayed, devastated, and angry. I had worked so hard for so long to realize my dream, and the Navy had thrown it back in my face.

In 1948, President Truman desegregated the Army and the Navy, but it had only been eighty-three years prior—one person's lifetime—that slaves had been emancipated, and it was still sixteen years before the passage of the Civil Rights Act. It would take time for Truman's groundbreaking decree to be fully implemented in the Navy, our nation's oldest branch of the military.

Fortunately, in 1947, President Truman established the US Air Force, through the National Security Act, ordering that it be desegregated from the start. I was in the right place at the right time. Because the Navy had rejected my application to flight school, I decided to explore my possibilities with the new branch.

Unbeknownst to the Navy Reserve, I enlisted in the United States Air Force in 1952 under the name of Alphonso B. Jones (my birth name is Alphonsus B. Jones) and was sent to basic training at Lackland Air Force Base, San Antonio, Texas. One of my first jobs was on a detail to mop the floors at the officers' club. When I mentioned to the white sergeant in charge that I was going to be an officer one day, he laughed like this was one of the funniest things he had ever heard. After I became an officer, I went back and greeted the sergeant, reminding him how I had worked for him mopping floors a few years back. He said he remembered me and that he never thought I could do it.

Within a month of graduating from basic training, I signed up for the entrance exam, passed the test, and was assigned to the Aviation Officer Candidate School, the precursor to our current Air Force Academy. At last, my dream was beginning to come true, and I would be forever grateful to the Air Force for giving me a chance to serve my country as an officer—an honor the Navy seemed unwilling to bestow on black men at the time.

As soon as I was accepted into the Air Force aviation school, I sent the Navy a copy of my orders, requesting a discharge from the Navy Reserves (since they didn't want me in *their* air corps). With my determination to fly, I was a bit of a hot potato, and I think they were glad to be rid of me. I received an honorable discharge from the Navy Reserve "for the convenience of the government" dated the day I was accepted into the Air Force aviation school.

When I first arrived on the base, I was impressed seeing a group of young men walking around the base so sharp and spick and span. I asked who they were and was told they were men training to be officers. They even walked a special way and were never seen moving in a relaxed manner or running anywhere. I wondered if I could be trained to be as disciplined as they were if I were accepted into their ranks. I had to work hard to meet their standards. Those who did not were "washed out" of the officer training program.

In many respects, the Air Force aviation school was like a finishing school for men. We learned how to wear our uniform, how to walk, talk, eat, sit, and so many other things that made us into an elite group called "officers." We had to remove any loose threads on our uniforms, and at our daily inspection, superior officers checked to make sure these "cables" were cut off. They also checked that we had on a pristine, properly creased uniform and that our ties and belt buckles were worn in a standard manner. Our shoes had to be highly polished daily. We learned how to give commands and lead men and how to conduct ourselves as representatives of our country and the United States Air Force.

The task was daunting, and I wondered if I would be able to rise to the challenge. I was willing to give it my best effort. If I could successfully complete the program, I would then go on to flying school and earn a commission as Second Lieutenant. I was grateful that the US military was giving me this opportunity. I made a commitment to do my very best.

Shortly after I arrived on the base, I met a fellow incoming black cadet named George Lomax. George was soft-spoken and knowledgeable and had a studious air about him. We became fast friends.

While the cadet program was "integrated," there were only a total of five or six black cadets out of a total population of maybe two hundred. A few of us were incoming, and a few were upperclassmen. As we ran into one another, we became friends.

One day, George and I were having lunch in the main dining hall when suddenly someone yelled, "Cadets, ten-hut!" We all snapped to attention at once, wondering what was going on. Imagine our surprise when a black man walked through the room to his reserved chair, where he sat with his staff and said, "At ease," and everyone sat back down.

I asked in amazement, "Who is that guy?!"

George replied, "That is Cadet Colonel William Crouch. He is the cadet commander in charge of the entire cadet corps. His job is to look out for the welfare of all of the cadets on the base."

I exclaimed, "Get out of town! We've got to figure out how to meet that guy!"

This turned out not to be as simple as it sounded because, as underclassmen, we were under strict guidelines regarding how to interact with senior officers. We knew that we would need to find an informal setting where we could strike up a conversation and not be in violation of the code of conduct for new cadets. We felt certain that if we found the right environment, he would be receptive.

We began to hang around the base exchange because we'd come to the conclusion that it was the only place where we could all be completely relaxed and informal. Finally, our paths crossed.

George was timid and bashful while I was brash and assertive; so, I made my approach, saying, "Colonel Crouch, we're new cadets, and we've been wanting to meet you. We just arrived on base a few months ago."

He greeted us warmly and asked where we were from, and we had a very nice conversation. What we didn't know at the time was that part of his job was to have a relationship with all two hundred of the cadets on the base so that if there were any problems, the cadets would bring them to him. This was an essential function of the cadet commander role. We just were happy to meet him.

I started a cadet drill team. I thought about the great drill team I could create with the sharpest and smartest cadets in the Air Force. I mentioned the idea to a group of my classmates, who were willing to give it a try. In a short time, we were ready. I got advice from one of our instructors, who suggested we wear a white cover over our dress brim hats, along with white gloves and scarves as part of our drill team uniform. He had us audition before a panel of officers that included the school commander. They were excited over the idea of our cadet drill team leading the march of the entire cadet corps in the next base parade and performing special maneuvers that I learned from a book about the Queen of England's special drill team. I was promoted to cadet captain, and we were invited to perform at all the base parades. I kept pushing myself to the limit of my ability. I was always grateful that the Air Force took my ideas seriously and allowed me the room to grow. This support followed me throughout my career.

After completion of the Aviation Officer Candidate School, George Lomax and I were sent to the same Cadet Flying School at Ellington AFB, San Antonio, Texas. We were given tests to see if there were any physical problems that would disqualify us from flying. I failed the eye test and was disqualified for pilot school. I was told that I had a condition called "atmospheric apparition," which means that I have trouble gauging the distance of an object, which could impact my ability to land a plane safely. I was disappointed, but I wasn't crushed because they immediately suggested an alternative that would allow me to fly. I could become a navigator. I passed all the tests that qualified me for the navigation school at James Connally Air Force Base in Waco, Texas. In 1951, the base was converted to an academic and flight training facility for navigators who were slated for eventual assignment to the Strategic Air Command. My friend Cadet George Lomax and I went into training together at Waco. I graduated with high potential and was promoted to Second Lieutenant, Navigator.

Master navigators were always in demand and in short supply. So, of course, I decided to become one. I wanted to be one of the very best navigators in the Air Force. I knew I had reached this goal when high-ranking officers started recommending me for difficult missions for which only the best were considered. And when they came up with the idea of refueling bombers mid-air so that they could bomb a target anywhere in the world, they started looking for the best navigators who could deliver 100-percent accuracy every time. The top brass started putting together a short list of officers who could get the job done, and my name was on the list. I was the only black officer included on it.

Word got around. Lieutenant Jones? He's damn good! The best we got! These words were even written down on a list of airmen given to the commander to guide his selection of his crew—praise I was unaware of until the day of our first mission when the aircraft commander teased, "Al, are you really that good?" to which I had to answer in truth, "Yes, sir. I am. That's why I am here with you. You asked for the best, and I am among the best we've got."

The other aircraft commanders I flew with repeated the joke. After flying with me for a few weeks, some event would inevitably prompt them to say, "You know, you're the damn best I have ever seen. I didn't believe it until I saw it with my own eyes." I always thought what he really meant was, "You are the best *black* navigator I have ever seen." But you take what you can get.

A general asked me why I was so driven to be among the best. He said, "It's got to be hard to keep up." Growing emotional, I said, "The Navy turned me down. I am glad the Air Force took a chance on me, to see what I could do, and I will always give everything I have out of appreciation."

I was assigned to Altus AFB in Oklahoma in 1954. When I arrived at the Altus airport in regular clothes, waiting for a staff car to pick me up, I saw an old man who looking around like he was lost or confused. He was shabbily dressed, about my size, but heavier.

I asked, "Can I help you?" He said I could and that he was looking for the Majestic Hotel. I looked in the phone book, but I couldn't find anything, and said, "There's no Majestic Hotel listed."

He took out a large wad of cash and began to explain why he was looking for the Majestic Hotel, and I said, "Put that money away! Don't show that much money in public!" I told him to convert his cash into a cashier's check and change just enough into traveler's checks to get him back home. Then I showed him my own traveler's checks.

"Where do you live?" I asked him.

"Alabama. My pappy died, and he gave me this money," he said.

As we were talking, the old man distractedly stopped another man walking out of the airport to get a cab, again, pulling out his wad of money. The newcomer then pulled me to the side and proceeded to try to get me to help him con the old guy's money from him.

Wanting nothing to do with the scheme, I told the old man that I was going to go back into the airport and find a police officer to help him. I waved down the first policeman I found, explaining that there was an old man with a fistful of money who appeared to need help.

"Which way?" he said excitedly. I pointed toward the airport exit I had come in from, and he took off running in that direction! I followed in close pursuit, but by the time we reached the spot where I had been talking to the two men, they had both disappeared.

Laughing, the officer told me, "Those two rascals were working a con game on you to cheat you out of your money! The way it works is that the second man talks you into putting the old man into a cab where you can rob him. But what really happens is the cab driver is in on the con, and they rob you." The police officer went on to say, "You must be honest, because the con only works on dishonest people." They were very good at what they did because I never suspected a thing.

While stationed at Altus AFB, I was sent to Elmendorf AFB, Anchorage, Alaska, to learn Arctic navigation over the North Pole. Altus AFB and Elmendorf AFB were both part of the classified mission to refuel airplanes in the air. We were sent to Alaska for special training, where we wore special warm clothes for weather twenty degrees below zero in the winter. It stayed dark for nearly twenty-four hours during that month of the year. (In June, it was the opposite: nearly twenty-four hours of daylight.)

Our heavy winter gear protected us from the elements, and I wore special goggles to protect my eyes. The cloth over my nose and mouth collected ice crystals. I had to move slowly to keep from overheating under my clothes. If I started sweating, I had to go inside and change my underwear to keep the sweat from turning to ice.

Once, I flew a mission to the North Pole and back using special electronic navigation equipment. The pilots became frightened when the compass needle started spinning. They had never seen a compass spin like that. As part of my navigator training, I knew that the compass would *always* behave this way near the North Pole. The purpose of the flight was for me, as navigator, and the pilots to experience polar navigation near the magnetic north, firsthand. Once we flew past the North Pole, the needle slowly came back into proper operation. The pilots had great respect for my navigation skills after that.

Life in Alaska involves certain dangers that you don't have to worry about elsewhere. Elmendorf AFB was in the middle of nowhere, and there were no fences defining the perimeter of the base or keeping wild animals out. Directly adjacent to the buildings were large, wooded areas on all sides. One day while I was out walking on base, I felt the hairs on the back of my neck rise, but as I looked around, I saw nothing amiss. My mind went into alert status, and I thought, *Am I in trouble? Am I being stalked? By what? A bear? A wolf? Maybe.* I started to reason my way through the situation. A bear or a pack of wolves would have made enough noise at a distance to alert me to run safely to a building. I began to suspect it was a lone wolf on my scent—likely one too old to run with the pack, who now had to hunt alone.

What to do?! Run? No, anything stalking me could catch me before I reached safety. I still could not see the wolf, but I could now hear the sound of branches breaking as he approached my location. I began to realize that I was too far out to make a run for the closest building and would need to somehow distract the wolf to allow myself a few seconds more to make the run. I started picking up rocks, thinking that if the wolf showed himself, I would throw rocks and scare him away.

The wolf came into view, and I made a short charge toward him and threw the rocks I had gathered at its face, shouting for help. A couple of the rocks landed, striking the wolf's snout and causing it to yelp like a frightened dog. I immediately turned and began running toward the building. All of the commotion attracted a few GIs in the building who immediately grabbed their rifles and raced out to help me.

I ran into the building and to safety as my rescuers ran past me, chasing the wolf and killing it. Later, they said I had done everything right, but that walking in Alaska can be dangerous to your health. They also said, "You'd have to be an idiot to walk around Alaska without a rifle." My answer: "You got that right!" The funny part was I was actually a trained marksman—I just hadn't carried a weapon because I hadn't known any better.

I returned to Altus Air Force Base in Oklahoma to continue my training, but soon I had to deal with a problem of a different sort. Some of our enlisted men came to my office with a problem. They said that in the segregated town, there were not enough homes on base or in town for black families, though there were plenty of lovely homes in town for white families. As the first black officer ever assigned to Altus Air Force Base, they thought I was in a position to exert some influence.

Right away, I called the Junior Chamber of Commerce and asked to speak at their next meeting. I asked if the city was planning on building a black home development as the black military community was struggling with a severe housing shortage. I told them that black members of the military were paid the same as white members and could afford good housing.

"Our 'Nigras' are very happy with the way things are!" one lady piped up.

"No, they're not," I said. I explained that I had met some of the leaders of the black community in town. They wanted better housing too. They would not tell her their true feelings because they did not want to lose their jobs.

I was so angry, I got up and left the meeting. I can't stand stupid people.

A friend in town called that afternoon and told me not to come back to town after dark. I lived on base, so I felt safe, despite the warning. Meanwhile, I sent a copy of my report about the incident to a high-ranking friend in Washington and asked him to see that President Truman got it. My sister, Beulah, worked in the White House answering and sorting the mail. My report was put on the president's desk.

The Air Force sent a special team to Altus to check out the housing situation mentioned in my report. The following week, I received orders transferring me to Bergstrom AFB, Austin, Texas. Clearly, the Air Force was concerned for my safety. Years later, I visited Altus and saw that excellent housing had been built for black local and military families. An officer is supposed to do all he can for the welfare of his men and their families. I was happy to see the concerns I had raised had, eventually, been addressed.

Bergstrom AFB was designated as a Strategic Air Command base within the military and housed many critical, top-secret activities. I arrived a few days early to get settled in before my start date. I drove through the gates to enter the base in a brand-new Ford convertible (my present to myself for my promotion to Second Lieutenant). I was dressed in civilian clothing. The guard on duty glanced at the military ID card I offered and casually waved me through. I drove a few feet, then slowly came to a stop, shaking my head, and reversed the car back through the gate.

I addressed the guard harshly: "Stand at attention, airman!" He immediately snapped to attention.

"Do you realize you are in gross dereliction of duty?" I exclaimed. "Either you failed to render proper courtesy to an officer or you failed to accurately read the identification I presented. Which is it?"

The guard began to stammer out a response, but I interrupted him. "Do you know what would happen if I reported this infraction? This is a highly classified facility and laxity this morning is inconsistent with base protocol and entirely unacceptable. I will not tolerate insubordination or mediocre performance! Do you understand me?" And I drove on through the gate onto the base.

I knew full well that I was likely the first black officer the guard had ever seen, but failure to salute an officer, in or out of uniform, is a serious breach of military courtesy. I also knew that other black officers were being transferred from Altus, Oklahoma to Bergstrom and believed it was important to establish from the get-go that we would not tolerate being treated differently than any other similarly ranked officer.

The military was a unique integrating institution in America at this time in our nation's history. It was a "society within a society" that operated according to its own unique hierarchical code. Where you stood in the hierarchy was broadcast to all, via badges and insignia on your uniform, and was clearly indicated on the military identification you carried with you at all times. Rank was the great equalizer. It shredded the norms of race relations prevalent in the broader society by superimposing a new framework for accruing, distributing, and demonstrating authority and respect. The rules for how junior and senior military personnel were to interact were clearly codified in handbooks that detailed proper military protocol. Infractions were punishable within the closed society's disciplinary system. The playing field was still not entirely level, promotions could still go to the candidate who "felt like a better fit," but the day-to-day racial microaggressions supported in the broader society were not tolerated in the military. Young black men, such as myself, joined the military in droves for the opportunities for career advancement and skill acquisition that were on offer, but often stayed for the benefits of working in an environment where, for the first time, racial prejudice was not tolerated as a matter of official policy.

When I reported to duty to my commanding officer, he looked at me sternly and said, "Oh, so you are the one who is causing so much trouble. The whole base is in an uproar! You chewed out a gate guard and word has gotten around that you are not taking any @#%$ from anyone." I swallowed hard and waited for him to continue. "By the way, you were entirely correct to reprimand that gate guard, Lieutenant Jones. Security protocols on this base are critical, given the strategic nature of our work." I sighed with relief that my superior officer, and by extension the US military, had my back, once again. When I rose to leave his office, he looked up at me with a sideways grin and said, "You're a feisty little fellow, aren't you?" I just smiled and continued on my way.

My mission at Bergstrom was to be prepared at any moment to refuel bomber aircraft anywhere in the world, over the ocean, so that they could fly on to bomb a Russian target. The KB29 plane I flew was developed to solve the problem of refueling long-distance bomber aircraft. When the B29s first came out, they could fly higher, further, faster, and with more bombs than any plane the Germans had. The US was very successful in bombing German airfields and factories and dominating the skies. But by the mid-1950s, the B29 had become obsolete as a bomber and was modified to become a refueling aircraft and rechristened the KB29. The KB29 could carry aircraft fuel for air-to-air refueling on a grand scale. With the KB29, we could fly so far that we sometimes utilized two crews—one that worked while the other slept on the plane.

There was no room for error in air-to-air refueling. Accuracy needed to be 100 percent because the bombers we met were always very low on fuel. We performed mid-air refuels again and again, never knowing if we were participating in a live engagement or simply a training exercise. Either way, the planes we were refueling were actually low on fuel, and so the mission was critical. Fortunately, our country never had to use this capability on a wartime footing—but we were ready.

LOVE AT FIRST SIGHT

1955 was the year Rosa Parks refused to give up her bus seat to a white man in Montgomery, Alabama. It was a time when the Reverend Martin Luther King Jr. was starting to emerge as a great leader fighting for equal rights. Progress was slow, but we were, indeed, making it.

Like many places in the US at that time, the city of Austin, Texas was plagued with racial injustice and highly segregated. I remember, one day, my friend Melvin Peeples drove by and invited me to join him and two blonde women for a drive. I said thanks, but declined, saying I had an appointment. I just thought that driving with two blonde women in a car wasn't a good idea in a segregated Texas city. I felt no need to go looking for trouble.

Despite segregation, Austin was a great place to live. It had a large black community, the Huston-Tillotson University, and many black restaurants, stores, and bars. My fellow black officers and I took evening courses at the university and met the local students. We attended the university dances and were very popular.

One day, I saw a beautiful young student walking across campus, and my life hasn't been the same since. The campus was full of beautiful young women. I don't know why I was so attracted to this particular one, but it was love at first sight. This young co-ed was slim and had a fair complexion, with hazel eyes and light brown hair. I caught sight of a beautiful smile and thought I'd be the happiest and luckiest person in the world if I could see that smile for the rest of my life.

I found out that she was friendly with a young man named Foxy, a very popular guy on campus. "Friendly" was about all she could be because I later found out that her father drove her to school each day and picked her up after her classes were over. Foxy was about my height, with an easy manner. I knew that Foxy was interested in hanging out with the young officers in town. We were both from Washington, DC. I had a car and a house, and he wanted to be friends.

I approached Foxy and asked him if he knew this beautiful young woman, I had seen walking across campus. He said, "Oh, yes. Her name is Muriel Warren, and she lives on a dairy farm." He was actually more interested in being friends with me than hanging out with Muriel, if you can imagine that.

The next time I saw her, I said, "Hi, Miriam!"

"My name is Muriel," she said shyly with a soft Texas accent and walked on down the street. I would have to do better than that.

Muriel had an older sister, Jeffrey, who was married to a sergeant named Archer. I looked Sergeant Archer up and asked him if he knew someone who would rent me a room in town. He said he had a house and that his wife was away at college, so he had plenty of room. So, I moved in with Archie and bided my time, waiting for him to invite me out to his wife's family farm.

In the meantime, I read books on milk cows so that I would be ready to impress Muriel's father when the time was right. At long last, Archie invited me out to the farm. I knew Muriel would be there. Archie introduced me to the family, and her father, Otho B. Warren, took me on a tour of his dairy farm. Mr. Warren was my height, was in excellent health, and had a sunny disposition. I liked his easy manner and great smile.

Mr. Warren was a successful businessman who owned fifty acres in Travis County, Texas and operated a dairy farm containing between fifty and one hundred cows that supplied Superior Dairies with milk. He was also the chef at Breckenridge Hospital and the owner of a restaurant. He was an educated man who taught adult education at night at the Pilot Knob School. He was known locally as 'Fessor Warren. Otho was a hard worker but always wore a smile and appeared to enjoy life very much.

While on the tour, I asked him about his milk yield per cow.

"You know about dairy cows?" he asked, surprised.

"A little," I said modestly. (That was true.) And just like that I was "in" with Mr. Warren.

When we got back from our tour of the farm, he handed me a can of beer. I didn't even drink beer but I drank that one happily.

Archer had told Muriel's parents that I was one of the new black officers on base. Mrs. Warren clearly thought I would be a good "catch" for her youngest daughter, Muriel. Mrs. Warren was a beautiful woman in excellent health with straight black hair that she wore pinned up in a pleasing arrangement. She had a medium build and very fair skin because her grandfather was white. Muriel's parents did not know that Muriel and I had already met.

The visit went well and I was invited back. The next time I visited, Muriel greeted me with an apron around her waist and a wooden spoon in her hand, as if to suggest she had cooked the meal, but I could tell by the way Mrs. Warren was checking on the progress of the food that she had done the cooking. After all, my mother had taught me how to cook, so I knew about these things. I thought to myself, *This child can't cook…but what the hell. I can hire a cook.*

When I next saw Muriel on campus, I approached her and struck up a conversation. "Hi, Muriel, how are you?" I asked, making sure I pronounced her name properly.

"I'm just fine," she said.

"Would you like to go out to the movies sometime?" I asked.

"Yes, but you have to check with my parents first," she replied.

"Well, I'll just come on out to the farm and see them," I suggested.

I drove out to the farm the next evening. Mr. Warren was not there, but Mrs. Warren welcomed me warmly and cut me a slice of pecan pie. I asked her, "How did you know this was my favorite kind of pie?" I probably would have said that no matter what kind of pie she had served me, but pecan actually was my favorite. As she piled a scoop of vanilla ice cream on top of my slice, I remarked, "This pecan pie is so fresh-tasting." She said, "The reason it tastes so fresh is because we have our own wild pecan trees on the farm." I was sold!

After a while, I said, "Do you think it would be okay if I took Muriel out to the movies sometime?"

She said, "Well, that would be just fine."

Muriel and I began dating with her parents' blessing, and many more visits and delicious homemade meals followed. Muriel's mom spoiled me to no end, preparing special dishes that she knew I liked. Muriel told me that her mom and dad liked me very much, and I got along with them very well.

One of our first dates was to a drive-in movie about an hour away. By the time the film was over, Muriel had fallen asleep. I drove back to the farm. After an hour, I didn't recognize the area, so I woke Muriel up.

I said, "Muriel, I don't recognize this area. We should be at your house by now."

Muriel answered, "Al, you are going the wrong way. How long have you been driving?!"

I said, "About an hour."

Muriel exclaimed, "Oh, my goodness, it's going to take us two hours to get back to the farm from here. We are going to be really late! I am in big trouble. We have to think up something to tell my parents that they will believe!"

I said, "No, we are going to tell them the truth."

Muriel cried, "Nobody's going to believe the truth!"

"I can't help what they believe, but I'm going to tell the truth. You fell asleep in the car and I took a wrong turn and ended up driving an hour out of the way." After a few minutes, I asked nervously, "What about your father? Do you think your father will be waiting for me with his shotgun?" I was never so acutely aware of what it meant to be in Texas bringing a farmer's daughter home two hours late.

Muriel replied, "He hasn't got a shotgun."

I suspected she was only trying to relieve my fears.

We got to the farm and both of her parents were standing outside the house. Mercifully, Mr. Warren was not, in fact, holding a shotgun, but he did have a belt strap in his hand. With my heart pounding, I explained what had happened, and to Muriel's great surprise, her parents believed me. They had been scared to death for our safety. They thought we had been in an accident, or worse, a run-in with locals who didn't like the idea of a black man driving a brand-new car.

I was relieved that her parents believed me because by that time, I had secretly decided I was going to marry Muriel, and I didn't want to do anything to mess things up with her parents. I was just waiting until we knew each other better to pop the question.

I had been shy around girls all my life. I was so busy working toward my dream of traveling around the world all those years that I really hadn't given girls much thought. For the first time, I was in love. I found someone I wanted to spend the rest of my life with. I was as surprised as anyone by this turn of events. I thought about her all the time, and for the first time, my dream expanded to include her. I needed her in my life or it would no longer have meaning.

One evening after a date, we found a location not far from her house where we could park the car and talk and kiss.

I said, "Muriel, my dream is to travel the world as an officer in the US Air Force. I want you to come along with me on this adventure. Will you marry me?"

Muriel smiled coyly and said, "Yes! What took you so long to ask?"

I asked, "Do you think your father would approve?"

Muriel said, "Oh, yes. Daddy likes you very much. I'll set up a meeting with him, and I'll call you and let you know when you can come by to ask him yourself."

When the appointed day and time arrived, as I drove out to the farm, I was surprised to realize how nervous I was, and my head was filled with thoughts of what I should say to convince Mr. Warren to give me his precious daughter's hand in marriage.

When I arrived, Mr. Warren was sitting down in the kitchen drinking a beer, and he smiled in greeting, which gave me a glimmer of hope.

I said, "Mr. Warren, I want to marry your daughter, and I want you to know that I love her and will take care of her for the rest of her life."

Mr. Warren paused and said, "I am okay with that, but I need for you to promise me one thing. I want Muriel to complete her college studies here in Austin and graduate with her degree."

I replied, "Of course."

He handed me a beer, and that was that. I drank the second beer of my life sitting in his kitchen, and I almost liked it. After a moment, he called Muriel in and told her he had given permission for us to marry. She smiled and gave me a big hug and kiss.

To my surprise, Muriel had been studying with Father Dayberry to become a Catholic for some time. She had secretly set her sights on me all along. Muriel and I were married on April 14, 1956, at Holy Cross Catholic Church.

My parents drove down from Washington for the wedding. I think they were relieved that I had found someone special since I had been so driven and obsessed with my career that I had never had time for girls before.

Muriel's father took them on a tour of Austin at night. He liked to yank people's chains. He told my parents before the wedding that he was going to attend in a clean pair of overalls and dye the gray in his hair with Easter-egg coloring. He, of course, had already rented a tux.

I had invited my all-white military crew to attend our all-black wedding in the heart of an all-black community in Texas. Their presence created a bit of a stir because, while the US Air Force was fully integrated at this time, Texas was not. In 1956, if you were to walk through Austin, Texas, you would have seen "whites only" signs at restaurants, hotels, pools, and water fountains.

Bergstrom Air Force Base, however, had been fully integrated since 1948. I had been assigned to a racially integrated crew, and we had lived together, slept together, and relied upon each other to be ready to fly to any point on the earth at a moment's notice if our country called on us. We were truly a band of brothers. My crew included some of the most important people in my life, and I wanted them to be present at my wedding.

After an initial ripple of surprise as my white groomsmen arrived in full military dress uniform complete with sabers, sashes, and white gloves, the wedding proceeded without incident. At the conclusion of the service, my crew formed an honor guard outside with their sabers upheld, creating an archway Muriel and I walked through as we exited the church. This was a great honor they bestowed upon us to show their love and support for me as a fellow crew member. In many ways, this archway was a metaphor for how the military created a path forward into an integrated future for so many young black men such as myself.

Muriel and I held our wedding reception in the church hall. Family and close friends were invited back to the house for a party and cards. We were so happy that we had found one another. We were blessed.

After our honeymoon in Monterey, Mexico, Muriel and I moved into a beautiful home in Austin. I couldn't wait to come home after work every day. We just loved to be together.

My career in the military began to really accelerate as the Vietnam conflict heated up. During my first two years of marriage, I was reassigned to the 96th Air Refueling Squadron, which was part of the elite United States Strategic Air Command (SAC), commanded by General Curtis LeMay, to secretly fly bombers nonstop from bases in America anywhere in the world at a moment's notice and destroy any enemy that attacked us or our allies. His tanker planes could carry enough fuel to secretly rendezvous with the bombers and their fighter escort planes to make sure they had enough fuel on their return home.

I was at the right place at the right time for my career aspirations. Could I do my part? I was going to give it my best effort.

The Cold War was raging in 1953, and I was part of a top-secret scheme of air-to-air refueling of B52 bombers with a range of 8,800 miles, far superior to the B25's range of 3,000 miles. A few years later, we had the B36, which had a range of 9,941 miles! We liked it so much, we built a total of 384 B36s! I was training to navigate tanker planes to rendezvous with the bombers. I set a goal to become known as a Master Navigator who could get the job done.

PARADISE

In 1956, there was a high-level requirement for navigators at Hickam Air Force Base in Hawaii, which would not become a state until 1959. Bases from around the world were required to supply one highly trained navigator to fill the need. My commander at Bergstrom AFB was tasked with finding one navigator who would volunteer to fill his quota. I was praying that he would be successful in persuading those ahead of me to stay in Texas.

When he called me into his office, I explained that I wanted to volunteer and that I had always wanted to live in Hawaii. My wife was planning to teach school in Hawaii, so we would be able to afford to live there. I got the assignment! My commander told me that I was one of his best navigators and was qualified to fill the quota. In appreciation for a job well done, he had approved my reassignment. He wished me well and indicated that he was going to recommend me for promotion.

Muriel had completed college in Austin, but if she left with me to go to Hawaii, she would not be able to take part in the graduation ceremony. I said she could join me after the ceremony. She said no way—she wanted to leave with me. By then, Muriel was pregnant and did not want to fly, so I got permission to go by ship. We were assigned to the beautiful SS *Lurline*, the flagship of the Matson Line. We said goodbye to family and friends and embarked on our first adventure together. This was our first cruise, and we loved it! Our cabin was spacious and was cleaned daily. The meals were excellent, and each day, they provided a bulletin of all the fun activities aboard the ship. They played Hawaiian music and offered classes on Hawaiian culture. We could not wait to get to the Hawaiian Islands.

When we arrived on Oahu, we were met with a big celebration at the pier, where local girls were dancing in grass skirts to Hawaiian music, and as we left the ship, we all received flower leis from the dancers. A white couple from our new squadron greeted us with leis, too. Evidently, race relations on the island were very relaxed. We soon found out that there were many racial groups in Hawaii, and they all seemed to get along very well together. If you combined all the minority groups there, they were the majority.

I remember a few years later, Muriel and I were assigned to greet a white couple coming to the islands. We made them feel as welcome as our white greeters had made us feel when we first arrived. I suspect they were as surprised to be given leis by a black couple as we were to receive them from the white couple years before. What goes around comes around.

Upon arrival, Muriel and I checked into the Officer's Quarters at Hickam AFB. We had a couple of weeks to settle in and enjoy Hawaii before I had to report for work. In those early days in paradise, we spent time at the beach enjoying our wonderful new life. I remember visiting Waikiki for dinner and strolling down Kalakaua Avenue, the main tourist street, and stopping at an artist's kiosk. He was drawing charcoal pictures, and I had him draw a portrait of Muriel. He drew her in pastel charcoal colors on a light blue background, showing Muriel's lovely black dress and white carnation corsage. He captured her light blue-green eyes, red lips, and Mona Lisa smile perfectly. We loved it so much that we had it framed and have hung it in every home we have ever lived in. Every time I see it, I am reminded of our wonderful life together these past sixty-three years! We were so lucky to have found each other. Couples who love and need each other are the luckiest people in the world.

We began looking for a parish shortly after we arrived in Honolulu. We happened to discover the Our Lady of Good Counsel community at a Mass in the cafeteria of a public school at Pearl City Elementary School. A group of parishioners mentioned that they were building a new church. We met Father Francis Marzen, the pastor. Father Marzen was a tall, slim, gray-haired priest who had the skill of planning the building of a church, talking people into helping with the construction, and raising the necessary funds.

When Father Marzen asked me if I would help him build the church, I could see he was full of faith that it could be done. His enthusiasm was contagious. Father Marzen was not afraid to get his hands dirty too and mingled easily with future parishioners. I liked Father Marzen immediately, and so I began volunteering to offload the lava rocks that would be used to make the walls. We all worked many months until the church was built. It was beautiful. Later, they built a Catholic school for kindergarten up through eighth grade, which all three of our children would attend. I would spend almost forty years volunteering at Our Lady of Good Counsel.

Our first home on Oahu was a two-bedroom house in Waikiki not far from the beach. The day we moved in, our neighbors, Evelyn and Louie, came by to welcome us with leis and drop off plates of Hawaiian food. After they left, we enjoyed our first local Hawaiian meal. It was steamed pork and greens (that looked like spinach) wrapped in plant leaves, which we later learned was called "Lau Lau." It was delicious!

We became fast friends with Evelyn and Louie and shared our circles with one another. Evelyn was an expert on Hawaiiana and a professional docent who provided tours of local sites. She arranged private tours for us at locations such as Bishop Museum, Iolani Palace, and Queen Liliuokalani's summer home, to help us get to know the history and culture of our new home. She also introduced us to many prominent local Hawaiians who were also her friends, allowing us to be a part of her social network as newcomers.

In turn, we invited Evelyn and Louie to our parties and to military events on base, which was a new world for them. Muriel and I were very social and loved to entertain. At one of our parties, a distinguished guest arrived with his daughter, and suddenly he became the object of everybody's attention. A buzz rippled through the room, and people were walking over and greeting him.

Evelyn pulled me aside and asked, "Al, who is that?"

I told her, "Oh, that's Admiral Sam Gravely, the commander of the 13th Naval Fleet, and the first African American officer promoted to the rank of admiral. Let me introduce you and Louie." After I had introduced them, Evelyn said, "Al, you have such interesting friends.

I've never met an admiral before!" In response, I said, "Well, let me introduce you to another friend, and I introduced her to Colonel Felix Salvador, the first African American officer to be promoted commander of Schofield Army Barracks.

Evelyn and Louie's welcome would have been wonderful for anyone, but for a young black couple raised in racialized America, their enthusiastic friendship and complete acceptance was unexpected and priceless. We would remain friends for the rest of our lives.

Muriel and I were learning that in all of America, there was perhaps no place more racially integrated than Hawaii. The military reinforced and took advantage of this natural state of affairs, appointing several high-ranking African Americans into the highest leadership roles on the island. Hawaii provided the perfect environment for these talented individuals to function effectively, unfettered by the racial animus gripping the rest of the nation. Their presence was an important part of the military effort to transform its culture and showcased the excellence of diverse leadership.

You may be wondering how a lowly lieutenant would know high-ranking officers such as Admiral Gravely, the three-star admiral who commanded the entire 13th naval fleet in the pacific theater, or a full Army colonel such Colonel Salvador, who commanded one of the island's Army bases, Schofield Barracks. Well, when I arrived in Hawaii, I decided to see if there was a chapter of my all-black Alpha Phi Alpha fraternity I had joined at the University of Michigan on the island. In fact, there was a chapter, and I was surprised and delighted to see that Admiral Gravely and an old friend, Colonel Salvador, were members. If we had not had the same fraternity in common, it would have been highly unlikely that I would have met either man because we would not have traveled in the same circles.

Shortly after I joined the local chapter, I attended a meeting hosted by Admiral Gravely at his home, which happened to be on Ford Island, a private island in the middle of Pearl Harbor. A shuttle boat manned by Navy personnel picked up me and several other guests, checking our identification credentials carefully. Admiral Gravely's home was huge, really a small mansion, and there were people serving hors d'oeuvres and drinks throughout. I said to myself, "Boy, this guy really knows how to live." Admiral Gravely greeted us warmly at the door in civilian clothes and introduced himself using his first name: "Welcome, I'm Sam. Come on in." You would never have known that he was the admiral of the entire 13th naval fleet, the largest organization at Pearl Harbor. As an Alpha Phi Alpha brother, though, he was just "Sam."

The house was full of about thirty Alpha Phi Alpha fraternity members, all African American men, some military and some civilian. I had met a few of the brothers at prior chapter meetings and was pleased to see Colonel Salvatore there, whom I had met in a similar fashion. It was clear to me, watching Admiral Gravely work the room, that he was intent on making sure we all felt comfortable and were not intimidated by his rank or stature; he clearly enjoyed interacting socially with all of us.

When I had joined the Alpha Phi Alpha fraternity as a college student at Michigan, I had no idea of the professional and personal relationships it would facilitate later in my life. Institutions such as fraternities provided a critical way for young black men to connect with senior black officers across rank and seniority and enabled friendships and mentoring relationships to form in an informal way.

Within a year, Hawaii felt like home. We had a thriving social network and were deeply embedded in the community through my volunteer work at the church and our military family. I built such a reputation for service at our church that I became known as Uncle Al. I was accepted as a member of the "ohana," the family of the local people. Much later, when I was a senior citizen, the local teens called me Tutu Kane, which means beloved grandfather.

FATHERHOOD

On May 14, 1957, Muriel gave birth to a beautiful baby girl. She looked a bit like both of us. She was the most beautiful baby I had ever seen—and I was her father! I started crying, I was so happy. The nurse wanted to know our ethnicity.

We said, "We are black."

"Black and what else?" she asked.

"Just black," I replied.

Hawaii is a place of tremendous ethnic diversity. Many different races are intermingled there, and it's not all uncommon for people to rattle off a long list of ethnicities in their background. This has always been a bit of a challenge for African Americans in our country, as our slave ancestry has generally made it difficult for us to know what ethnicities have mixed and mingled to produce us. All we could say was that we were just "black."

I was so happy, I asked Muriel if I could name our baby daughter. I chose the name "Angela Leilani," which means "Angel of the Heavenly Flowers" in Hawaiian. We called her Angie. We spent hours just looking at her. I would sing to her "Sweet Leilani, Heavenly Flower, I dreamed of paradise for two. You are my paradise completed; you are my dream come true." I sang this song to her every day throughout her early life. We were overjoyed with our new daughter.

When Angie was a little girl, Muriel had her take ballet lessons. Angie would dance ballet around the house, and we would clap and say,

"Bravo! Bravo!" She was happy to be the center of attention. At Christmastime, we went to see *The Nutcracker* ballet, a terrific production. Angie was delighted with the music, the costumes, and the dancers twirling and jumping around the stage.

During intermission, Angie leaned over and whispered to me, "Daddy, Daddy! When do I dance?"

"You are not dancing in this ballet, honey," I replied. "We just came to watch." She folded her arms and said, "I'm ready to go home."

I looked over at Muriel and said, "We have a performer here," and we both smiled at our darling daughter.

Muriel gave birth to our second child on July 23, 1958—a baby boy! I had always wanted a son. We named him Alphonsus Beverly Jones, Jr. Immediately I thought about all the things my son and I could do together. We could join the Scouts and go camping.

Now we had a girl and a boy. Life could not be better. We soon realized that with a second child, we needed a larger house and purchased a home on Hoohaku Street in Pearl City.

One day, we were in the park and Baby Al wandered off on his own. Angie said, "Daddy, where is Baby Al going?" I said, "Go get him." She ran after him. He was just learning to walk, so she quickly caught him and took his hand to lead him back to us. He didn't want to go with her, so he snatched his hand away and tried to run. I said, "Muriel, watch this." I knew Angie would win the struggle. She patiently kept trying to take his hand and lead him back. He gave up and let her take him back to us. Angie was a good babysitter. We spent hours taking care of them and laughing at their antics as they tried to communicate with us.

The kids and I sometimes made a tent in the living room with a blanket and furniture and slept overnight in it, just like Muriel and me— before we had kids—would sometimes camp out on the beach on an air mattress and a blanket near a hotel in Waikiki with other local couples and listen to the music drifting over from a floor show. There were so many local couples that we were a safety net for each other.

I cherished my time with Angie and Al Jr., because during these years, for two weeks out of every month, I was often away flying missions in Japan, Okinawa, and Guam. We would fly supplies into military bases at these destinations and then return to Hawaii. These missions took two weeks because of crew rest requirements in the Air

Force. We could only fly a set number of hours a day, so when we landed at our first destination, we would "crew rest" for a few days, and another crew would take our plane on to the next destination. Once we were rested, we would take over for a newly arriving crew and take their plane onto its next destination.

Muriel had the hard job of taking care of Angie and Baby Al and the household while I was away. She did a wonderful job. On Sundays, the kids were dressed beautifully for Mass and everything was always in order when I returned from a trip. Nevertheless, my assignment was really hard on our new family. Muriel found her new responsibilities both scary and exciting. Scary, because she had really never been in a mixed-race environment before and because of the challenges of being a new young mother on her own, much of the time. Exciting, because she was learning that she could cope with all of these new responsibilities and was able to pursue her own ideas of how to get things done. I still wanted to see the world, but two weeks away flying every month for years was too much with a young family. I started planning to qualify for two desk jobs that would allow me to fly only one short trip a month.

When I would return from a trip, sometimes the kids would ask to do something, and I wouldn't know if Muriel was on board with their request. So, I would say, "Go ask your mother." I wanted her to know that I understood that my frequent absences meant she was in charge of setting the ground rules with the kids and that I supported her 100 percent. In this way, I sought to minimize the disruption of my comings and goings on the family routine.

Our daughter Angie also helped in her own way. She was very smart, tough for her age, and very protective of her younger brother. One time, I put Angie in charge of watching Baby Al in our yard. I told her not to let the other kids get too close. I looked out the window, watching to see how she would handle this responsibility. I saw her tell a boy bigger than her to "get back!" He didn't respond, and I was on my way out the door to intervene. Before I could get there, the boy was on the ground crying. She had pushed him with all her might and he fell back on the grass. He wasn't hurt. I gave her a hug for taking good care of her brother.

As young couples often do, Muriel and I fell into different roles as parents. Muriel was the day-to-day general, and I was the assistant and the "go to" guy for fun activities. I later realized this arrangement was not entirely fair, but my travel made it our default. Fortunately, we had great babysitters and went out a lot. One of our favorite spots was the officers' club at Hickam AFB. One evening, the waiter told Muriel that minors were not allowed in the bar. She looked so young and beautiful he thought she was my daughter! I laughed so hard and teased her about it mercilessly. (Years later, when she was teaching school in Waipahu, some of her students also thought I was her father!)

In 1959, Hawaii became the fiftieth state in the union. Public education on the islands significantly lagged the standard on the mainland. At Waipahu Intermediate School, where Muriel taught, the principal noticed that Muriel's students were outperforming those in other classes. When he asked Muriel about it, she told him her students were ahead of other classes at the school but were behind peer students on the mainland. She recommended that the school's teachers take classes at the University of Hawaii to learn how to bring our students up to par. Muriel said that our kids would have to learn to speak standard English in school instead of the pidgin English commonly spoken on the island. We had a long way to go, but we had to start somewhere, with the goal of providing the best education possible and preparing our students for future employment. The principal agreed and began having meetings to get everyone working together to make it happen. These educational gaps continue to challenge the islands to this day.

SURVIVING VIETNAM

In 1957, I was assigned to the 50th Air Transport Squadron, Military Airlift Command, Hickam AFB, Hawaii as a navigator on C-124 cargo aircraft. This assignment was different from my last assignment of always preparing to go to war. My new job would be to peacefully navigate from Hawaii across the Pacific Ocean to countries in Southeast Asia, carrying cargo and military personnel. The Air Force wanted me to become proficient in flying throughout the Pacific Ocean region.

What a difference from my last assignment! On my last base, I was always on alert to participate in wartime exercises. Now, I almost felt like a commercial airline crew member, peacefully transporting people and cargo without the stress of potentially going to war hanging over my head. When we arrived at each new destination across the Pacific Ocean, we always had a few days off before our next flight. This allowed me to tour these different locations and enjoy the local sights and culture. I was finally living my dream of seeing the world.

My flights from Hawaii took two weeks. I flew from Hawaii to Wake Island and remained overnight or longer. I remember leaving Hawaii one Saturday night, flying a few hours, and arriving on Wake Island on Monday! I flew over the International Date Line at 180 degrees longitude. The eastern side is one day behind the western side. On one trip, I was on Wake Island at a New Year's Eve party. We left and flew to Hawaii. The next morning, my wife said, "It's New Year's Eve. Let's go to a party!" I celebrated two New Year's Eves that year. When you fly west across the International Date Line, you lose a day. Flying east, you gain one.

Flying from Wake Island, there were many mission options. I have flown to all of these locations:

1. South to Eniwetok Island or Kwajalein Island or to Tinian Island. I flew to Tinian Island, which was the launching point for the atomic bomb attacks against Hiroshima and Nagasaki during World War II. I had read that there were three atomic bombs on the island, and only two were dropped. So, while I was visiting Tinian Island, I resolved to solve this mystery once and for all. One day, I set off to search for the third underground silo—and I found it! This means that if Japan had not surrendered after we dropped the second bomb, we would have dropped the third one.

2. West to Clark AFB, Philippines; or Taiwan, Formosa; or Hong Kong, China;

3. West to Saigon, South Vietnam; or Phnom Penh, Cambodia; or Bangkok, Thailand; or Seoul, South Korea.

I was on a list of master navigators who could be called on at any time to accomplish difficult missions, and eventually I was selected to replace a master navigator who had been injured in combat. My mission was to navigate three planes to the 38th parallel between North and South Korea, turn before crossing the 38th parallel, and drop Army paratroopers on the Han River Drop Zone.

By this time, my twin brother, Aloysius, had joined the military and was serving in the Air Force, as well. When I arrived at the Army briefing site, for my first mission, they said, "Jonesy, what are you doing back here?"

"I'm Captain Jones' twin brother," I told them. When the Army commanding general arrived, he said, "What is Jonesy doing up here?" This time, I played along with the gag and said, "I came back to give everyone some help." Everyone in the room laughed.

The general said, "There is clearly a joke here. What's the punchline?" I told him I was Captain Alphonso Jones, twin brother of Captain Aloysius Jones, who had been stationed there a few months ago. My brother was an Air Force commander at a radar aircraft early warning site.

One of the most memorable and important experiences in my career occurred in this assignment with the 50th Air Transport Squadron. The mission involved coordinating a paratrooper drop with our South Vietnamese allies. After the drop briefing, the Vietnamese colonel on the mission told the American commander of the mission that he and his men wanted to be dropped on a HALO, or a high altitude drop. The Vietnamese colonel was tall and slim with an overbearing attitude. As a colonel, he clearly felt superior to others of lower rank. He appeared to be a person who was accustomed to having his own way.

Instead of telling him it could not be done in the specified area during peacetime, the American mission commander told him the drop decision was up to me as the drop navigator. The navigator is responsible for surveying the area of a drop and deciding if the terrain and weather are safe. If there were high winds over the drop area, the drop would be canceled.

The Vietnamese colonel did not want to speak to me—maybe because of my race or maybe because of my lower rank. I was just a captain and not a lieutenant colonel. Whichever it was, the Vietnamese colonel told me that he and his men wanted to be dropped on a HALO and said that he had been told I could authorize the drop. I firmly told him, "No, sir. I will not be dropping any HALOs on this mission." Before I could tell him that it was too dangerous to do a high-altitude drop in that particular zone because of the tree line and the nearby river, and that, moreover, such a drop was against our regulations in peacetime, the Vietnamese colonel bellowed, "I am ordering you!"

I became incensed at this man's stupidity and lack of concern for the safety of his men. I knew that if I obeyed his order, some of his men would be killed or injured and the Pentagon would blame me.

Angrily, I said, "I tell you what, Colonel, I will take your *@&# to the moon and drop it there if you want me to, but I am not dropping your men on a HALO! Sir." Then I turned around and walked away.

The Vietnamese colonel was fit to be tied. He called the Pentagon to speak to the chief of staff for the US military, a four-star general, to complain about me. The military chief of staff consulted with the chief of the Air Force, who told him that that drop area was so dangerous for a high-altitude drop that we had a regulation prohibiting it in peacetime.

Armed with this information, the chief of staff for the US military told the Vietnamese colonel that I had made the correct decision. He said, "If Captain Jones had obeyed your order, many paratroopers would likely have been injured or killed in the drop. Captain Jones would surely have been court marshaled." As for my losing my temper with the Vietnamese colonel, he said that junior officers in command situations are human and sometimes get angry, just like anyone else. My American command chain backed me up 100 percent.

In fact, the chief of staff for the US military was angry with the mission commander, who had instructed the Vietnamese colonel to seek my authorization. The mission commander should have explained to the colonel why the HALO drop was disallowed instead of putting the responsibility of countermanding a senior officer's order on the shoulders of a junior officer. The chief of staff had a big laugh with his fellow officers about my willingness to drop the Vietnamese colonel's "butt" (though I had used a different word) from the moon. He recommended to the chief of the Air Force that I receive the Distinguished Flying Cross for a job well done in the interest of saving lives by disobeying a direct order from a superior officer, the Vietnamese colonel. It was approved and presented to me in 1972 when I retired.

While I was on temporary duty to Saigon, South Vietnam, we had a mission to transport Vietnamese prisoners to the prison at Vung Tau. Saigon was an exotic, chaotic city. To my eyes, the men walked around in clothing that looked like pajamas, and the women wore beautiful silk tunics over long, silk pants. Everyone rode on bicycles! If you were driving a vehicle, you had to be very careful to avoid the hundreds of bicyclists everywhere. Only the wealthiest members of society could afford to drive cars. The local people spoke broken English that was difficult to understand, but they were all very polite, and the food was plentiful, delicious, and cheap. I loved it!

At the start of our mission to transport Vietnamese prisoners to Vung Tau, the Army's military police (MP) loaded a large number of prisoners onto the plane and had them sit on the floor. There were only a few policemen, and the crew was concerned about our safety. We could have easily been overpowered by the prisoners.

"Captain Jones, put the fear of God in them!" the commander ordered. So, I took out my pistol and opened the back of the plane. The plane was designed to drop supplies strapped to rolling floor platforms out of the back. When it opened up, the cargo would slide out and float down to the ground by parachute.

I asked the military police on the mission to translate my orders to the prisoners in Vietnamese. I told the prisoners I didn't want any *@#& on my plane. "Put your hands under the floor platforms you are sitting on, and you will feel wheels to each floor platform. If I have any trouble, I'll open the back of the plane, release the floor locks, and tilt the plane into a climb, and you will all roll out! Those who manage to survive holding onto the side straps, we will shoot and throw their bodies out!"

I saw how frightened they were. I told the MPs that if there was any trouble to hold onto the straps on each side of the plane to keep from falling out of it.

By the time we arrived at the prison, the plane reeked with the strong odor of urine. The commander said, "Damn, Al, you overdid it. We have to wash down the plane floor before leaving here!"

Looking back on this experience now, it may seem that we were cruel and heartless to scare the prisoners the way we did. In fact, I did it to save their lives. Had the prisoners, many of them hardened soldiers, decided to rush us and attempt to take over the plane, we would have had to kill them all. War is hell.

Speaking of urine, I have another story that took place in South Vietnam. We had a mission to pick up a full load of people and carry them down to Saigon. The flight commander reminded me that we had three extra seats in the flight crew area. So, naturally, I went back and selected three cute nurses to come join us up in the crew compartment where the seats were more comfortable. I helped them put on their seat belts, offered them snacks and coffee, and told them that sometimes the weather was choppy, so they should stay in their seats with their belts fastened.

One of the nurses, Alice, heedless of my advice, left her seat to wander around the plane, and we hit some bad weather. She was so scared that by the time she got back to her seat, she had wet herself. What she saw was our plane entering dark clouds, turbulence, and thunder. I was busy directing the plane through the bad weather on the radar, which gave me a picture that helped me direct the plane through the path with the least turbulence.

When we arrived in Saigon, Alice told me about her problem. I got Alice's luggage, and she was able to clean up and change into clean dry clothes with the help of her two friends. I stood guard to give them privacy. I said they had to buy me lunch. They appreciated that Alice was able to change clothes on the plane without having to exit the aircraft in embarrassment.

We walked in the cafeteria, laughing like old friends. Making good on their promise, they said, "Al, what do you want for lunch?" They got my lunch and theirs and came back to join me at the table.

My crew looked flabbergasted. They said, "How does he do it? Look at this guy making time with these three beauties, and he is a married man!" I just laughed. I told the three ladies what they had said, and they laughed so hard. Our cover story was working. No one ever learned of Alice's "accident."

On my first trip to Tachikawa, Japan, I wondered what I would encounter. I remembered the stories when I was young about the sneak attack on Pearl Harbor on December 7, 1941. I also remembered reading that their Admiral Yamamoto, who led the attack, had actually advised against it, saying that attacking America was like grabbing a tiger by the tail. The tiger will turn and kill you.

And then there was the story of the Battle at Midway about six months after Pearl Harbor. We won the battle and destroyed four of their aircraft carriers, losing only one of our carriers. Colonel Doolittle's bombers sailed to Japan secretly on a Navy carrier and took off when they got close and bombed Tokyo. After the attack, the American bombers landed in China. The Japanese were shocked because their emperor had said that America did not have the capability to bomb Japan. They knew America, the tiger, was winning. And of course, there were the two bombs dropped on Nagasaki and Hiroshima that convinced them to surrender.

This had all happened years prior to my arrival in Japan, but I wondered how we would be treated. To my surprise, we were received very well, and I had a wonderful time. The dollar was strong against the yen, so I felt rich, and I bought great gifts for my family. I got a massage, and two cute girls came in wearing what looked like bras and panties and were all over my body. Don't get ahead of me—I just got a massage. They were walking all over my back. What an experience!

Once, I was on mission flying from Japan to Wake Island. The co-pilot woke me up to assist the working navigator who appeared to be in trouble. We were flying a long-distance mission over the Pacific Ocean and had two crews aboard, one working while the other slept. Navigation was entirely manual in those days; there were no computers. The working navigator, a major nearing retirement age, was on a skills re-qualification exercise. His recent calculations showed us moving further and further away from our destination. He became increasingly agitated, repeatedly checking his work, but, unsure if his calculations were accurate, had not taken any corrective action. Picking up on the working navigator's anxiety, the co-pilot woke me up.

I didn't know exactly what was going on, but I knew we were in a dangerous situation and needed to figure out where we were as quickly as possible. I rapidly calculated our position off of three stars visible in the sky, and realized that not only were we way off course, but we did not have enough fuel to go back to Japan and nor could we make it to Wake Island, our original destination.

I immediately informed the aircraft commander piloting the plane, a colonel, that we were in a state of emergency and would need to divert to Iwo Jima at once. Iwo Jim was a small island I believed we could reach, that was stocked with fuel for just this type of situation. The colonel was incensed that the working navigator had not alerted him of the emerging problem when there had been time to make adjustments and return to Japan.

I manually plotted a course to Iwo Jima, telling the pilot to turn to a heading of 195 degrees. The pilot broadcasted a "Mayday" alert, set the heading and called Iwo Jima, alerting them that we would be coming in to make an emergency landing for fuel. The pilot then checked a compass on the plane that automatically points to the location of where you place a call, to aid in navigation to that location. Amazingly, the radio compass needle turned to exactly 195 degrees, the precise heading I had just recommended. It was a coincidence—no one is that good—but the pilots thought I was, and I decided to let them believe it.

Iwo Jima stunk of sulfur. No one went there unless they were forced to. The pilot was still furious that the working navigator had put the entire crew at risk and had not even bothered to wake me for help when he first began to realize something was wrong. Had the problem been flagged earlier, we would have had plenty of time to validate his calculations, make heading corrections or return to Japan to offload some of our cargo and take on more fuel. I will never know if my race, rank (I was only a captain at the time) or age factored into the working navigator's reluctance to get my help, or if was simply a matter of pride, but if the co-pilot had not awoken me and we had continued off course, we would have reached a point where we would be too far to refuel anywhere. We would have simply dropped into the ocean when our fuel ran out.

After refueling at Iwo Jima, we flew on to Wake Island, where they confirmed that a massive jet stream had blown us off course. The colonel knew we had cheated death that day and my actions had saved the crew. The working navigator failed his recertification and was required to take more training before he would be permitted to fly solo. The aircraft commander later recommended me for an air medal for the decisions I made that day that saved the crew.

My reputation as a top-notch navigator began to grow. On one flight, as we were taking off, the aircraft commander said, "Jonesy, they tell me you're damn good. Are you damn good?"

"Yes, sir. I am a master navigator. That means I am among the best."

In my day, if you were black, you really had to put yourself out there to get any recognition. Black navigators were perceived in one of two ways: either "He doesn't really know what he is doing" or "He is damn good!" My reputation as being in the latter category had begun to precede me.

On this particular flight, I saw a small cloud up ahead. I checked my radar and saw that it indicated turbulence.

As we got closer, I told the pilot to go around it. The pilot looked at me with disbelief and said, "It's just a little cloud. We'll just go through it. It won't take but a few minutes." I said to myself, "I've got you now!"

I was expecting some turbulence that might spill his coffee, but we experienced something far worse!

As we approached the innocent-looking, little cloud, I went back to my seat and made a show of putting my things away in my bag and clipping on my parachute (I always wore my harness and only had to clip on the parachute pack to be ready to jump out of the plane if I had to).

As soon as we entered the cloud, we experienced heavy turbulence and a down-wind that dropped us about five hundred feet, like we were about to fall into the ocean! The commander spilled coffee all over his clothes. The two pilots pulled the controls as hard as they could to climb at max power. Within the next few minutes, we hit a strong upwind, and the plane jerked upward, climbing rapidly to a point higher than we were before. All this happened in less than ten minutes! I was frightened as much as everyone else. Who knew this little cloud would be that severe!

Afterward, I lit a cigar, and the nicotine calmed me down. I got out of my seat, walked up and stood between the commander and the co-pilot smoking on my cigar, as though nothing had happened. By then, the two pilots had the plane under control. They exclaimed, "What the hell just happened?!"

The commander cursed and said, "I got hot coffee all over my clothes! You told me to go around that cloud, Al! How did you know that would happen? We have been flying through little clouds for hours. How did you know there was so much turbulence in that one?"

I took a drag on my cigar and said, "They told you I was damn good, didn't they?"

To be fair, I had no way of knowing that that cloud had *that* much turbulence! Nobody could have known that, and I was as frightened as everyone else while our plane was tossed around so violently in the wind. But they didn't need to know that.

When I was at the officers' club that evening having a drink with my friends, I could hear the commander from all the way across the room, having one too many drinks with his buddies. The commander said, "See that captain over there? If you ever fly with him, and he wants you to fly around a little cloud, you better do it!" My friends wanted to know what happened, so I told them the story, and we had a good laugh.

Another time, we had a mission to carry visiting officials to Midway Island. I had heard about the Gooney birds there. I laughed at the way they flapped their wings to fly into the air and how when they wanted to land, they would begin running in the air as they slowed down, but then sometimes they would just fold up their wings, stop running, and tumble to a stop. It seemed like sometimes they just lost track of what they were trying to do, be it taking off or landing. I never got tired of watching the Gooney birds' antics. Once I walked up to one and put my foot out. He just bit it like it was a sandwich.

Sometimes we would fly a hospital plane full of wounded US military patients to Saigon, where they would be shipped on to hospitals near their hometowns in America. I felt sad to see so much misery. Our American military doctors and nurses provided excellent care to our wounded soldiers, but it was heartbreaking to see the damage the war had wrought. When my duties permitted, I sometimes would greet the patients and answer their questions about their long journey home. The nurses and doctors were terrific, but they were generally busy getting the wounded situated, and I sensed that many of the injured soldiers just wanted to talk to someone and be reassured that we were going to get them home.

Sometimes we flew those who died in battle to Saigon, sealed up in body bags, to be shipped back to the mortuary nearest to their homes. The first time I flew this type of mission, I found myself overcome with sorrow. I was not prepared for the tears that suddenly overwhelmed me. Many of my fellow crew members had the same reaction. I went up to my seat in the cockpit. I needed to pull myself together; I had a job to do. I will never forget the experience of transporting the wounded and the dead.

Some missions were in support of the Army. We flew helicopter fuel to dirt landing areas and offloaded it into underground fuel containers. With the help of jets attached to the sides of the aircraft in addition to our four engines, we would roar off the ground like a jet with the Vietcong firing rockets all around us trying to blow us up. This was our most dangerous type of mission. I was always terrified on these missions, but my training kept me focused on doing my job. I knew that if we were hit by enemy rocket fire, our plane would turn into a great ball of flame, and we would be killed instantly. I prayed to God to protect us. And somehow, He did. When we returned to the base after these missions, we usually headed to the officers' club and got drunk—anything to wipe out the memory of that harrowing experience.

Despite the occasional danger, I enjoyed all my trips to Southeast Asia. The only problem was having to be away from my family two weeks each month. After four years of this schedule, I decided I needed to make a change. I resolved to figure out how to qualify for a job as squadron commander or staff officer, which would allow me to spend more time with my family and have greater control over my flight schedule. In these positions, I would only need to fly four hours a month with some occasional longer duties. I would also be able to take college classes on campus or by mail. I had always intended to finish my college degree. This move would also mean I would be qualified to do three jobs and would have a better pick of future assignments.

In 1961, I was assigned to McGuire AFB in Trenton, New Jersey, as a navigator. I liked this job because I would be flying from the East Coast to Europe. We would also be able to take vacations to Muriel's home in Texas, to my home in Washington, DC, and to visit New York City. As an added bonus, my brother Aloysius just happened to be stationed at the same base. He greeted me and my family at the airport when we arrived and helped us get settled in. We were so glad to see each other! We had been separated for several years, which is tough on twins.

One day, while I was off flying to Europe, my brother invited Muriel and our two kids to join him on a trip to visit our mother in Washington. Even though no deception had been intended, Mother didn't realize it was Aloysius with Muriel and the kids and not me! They had a lovely visit, catching up on the news, until suddenly, at the end of the day, at dinner, Mother looked at Al and said, "You're not Alphonso! What are you doing with Alphonso's family?!" We looked and sounded so alike she did not discover the switch until dinner. My brother said he had just invited Muriel and the kids to join him since I was on a trip.

On that flight, my plane developed problems, and I had to return to McGuire. I drove to DC to join Muriel and the kids. When I got there, the kids were napping, and everyone was out shopping except my brother, who was babysitting. We decided to play a trick on Muriel. I put on Aloysius' clothes and sat in the living room watching TV. My brother waited upstairs. When they returned home, Muriel sat down next to me but did not recognize me. After a few minutes, Aloysius came down the stairs. Muriel ran over to the stairs to greet him thinking he was me. I said, "Don't hug him. I am your husband!" Everyone thought it was a funny trick—except Muriel. I apologized to her and promised to never play that trick on her again. And I never did.

Once in 1961, Aloysius invited Muriel and me to a party at his house. He was a bachelor and had great parties in those days. Muriel and I put our two kids to bed upstairs in his spare bedroom. We had a great time at the party, and since the kids were asleep when we were ready to go, we just left them there and planned to pick them up the next day.

At the time, Aloysius was dating a girl named Helen and trying to impress her. She had stayed the night and was sitting in the kitchen with him and a couple of his roommates in the morning when two kids came running downstairs and into Aloysius' arms, shouting, "Daddy! Daddy!" My own kids had trouble telling us apart, but Al quickly corrected them and said, "I'm not your father!"

Helen said, "I thought you said you weren't married."

"I'm not!" he said.

Helen asked Angie (five years old) and Al Jr. (four years old), "Is this your father?" They looked at Al and solemnly nodded.

Helen said to the room at large, "He is disowning his own children—and they look just like him!"

Finally, one of Aloysius' friends got him off the hook, explaining that the kids belonged to his twin brother and that he and his wife had left their kids in a spare bedroom the night before. Everyone laughed and thought it was great fun.

During that same year, I flew temporary duty to Rio De Janeiro, Brazil; Bermuda Island; Azores Island; Lisbon, Portugal; Madrid, Spain; Thule, Greenland; Reykjavik, Iceland; Paris, France; Frankfurt, Germany; Rome, Italy; Rotterdam, Amsterdam; Athens, Greece; Cairo, Egypt; Adana, Turkey; Tel Aviv, Israel; and Riyadh, Saudi Arabia. My dream had come true; I was flying all over the world.

I also completed the Squadron Officer School at Gunter AFB, Alabama. I was now qualified for two jobs. My chances of being sent back to Hawaii were good.

In 1962, Muriel got pregnant with our third child. She was feeling a bit blue, so I said, "Let's go to Paris! We will visit the Christian Dior fashion house, go to a fashion show, and I'll buy you a new hat there." She immediately perked up, and so we flew to Paris and had a wonderful time. And we actually did buy a hat. When anyone admired that hat, she would proudly say, "We flew to Paris to get it."

Meanwhile, Aloysius was also enjoying life. By this time, he was living in Germany, where he had met a beautiful young German woman named Elizabeth at an exhibition for his painting. Aloysius had always been a gifted painter, and in fact, we had been holding a number of his paintings in our home, which we sent to him for this German exhibition. Elizabeth was an artist too. She was tall, blonde, and beautiful, and with her slender build could have easily been mistaken for a model.

After dating for a while, they decided to get married. They had to get permission from the Air Force in order to get married in Germany, a complicated process that got caught up in the political red tape of American GIs marrying German girls. Things were tough in Germany in those years, and there was a belief that some German girls were taking advantage of GIs to obtain US citizenship. Al and Elizabeth finally decided to just get married in America, which was fairly straightforward. I resolved to help my brother find a Catholic church for their wedding and obtained approval from the chaplain of the church on McGuire AFB.

Elizabeth and Al flew in from Germany, and our immediate family drove up from Washington, DC. It was a wonderful wedding! We all drove back to DC so Elizabeth could meet the rest of the family. Elizabeth was surprised to see just how large our family was since she was from a small family. Al and Elizabeth flew back to Germany after honeymooning in Washington.

Our daughter, Kimberly Ann, was born on September 5, 1962, at McGuire AFB, New Jersey. We had thought our lives were perfect, but, oh, my, what a wonderful gift! Kim was a beautiful, happy baby. She was like a living baby doll, and we all wanted to play with her. Angie was five years old, and Al Jr. was four. Angie was like a second mother to Kim; we even let Angie feed her. Muriel and I were so happy to have darling Kim in our family.

Kim had an immense fondness for animals. She would pet any animal that stood still enough for her to walk over and touch. She loved horses, dogs, cats, sheep, goats, cows, etc. One day, I took her up on my horse for a ride in the park. She was so happy! The horse suddenly started to run down the trail. I was holding her tightly and trying to rein the horse down to a walk. Finally, I got it under control. I thought Kim would be scared (I know I was). She just clapped her little hands and said, "Do it again, Daddy! Do it again!" I said to myself, "We've got a horseback rider here."

Kim always felt excited about everyday experiences. Our housekeeper loved Kim so much she was willing to babysit all three of our children anytime we asked her just to be with Kim.

Meanwhile, my international adventures continued as I flew to some of the world's most fascinating cities. When I went TDY (temporary duty travel) to Rio, Brazil, our crew spent a week touring around. I saw a voodoo ceremony in the park. The voodoo leader was a slim man dressed only in a pair of white pants and a red cape. There were several assistants standing around him in a circle holding candles. A dead chicken lay on the ground in front of the leader. I was watching the ceremony from a bridge and asked, "What's that going on down there?" My guide quickly tried to lead me away, saying, "Voodoo, no good, no good." This only whetted my appetite to move closer to see exactly what was going on. I had my guide approach the leader and ask permission for me to observe the ceremony. There were all sorts of incantations; the chicken's head was cut off, and so forth.

After the ceremony, to thank them for letting me observe the ceremony, I gave the leader a Polaroid picture I took of him, but I had forgotten to apply the fluid needed to stop the photo from overdeveloping. The blank picture first developed into a picture of the leader, but then the picture slowly turned black. This terrified the leader! He thought I was a witch doctor from North America who placed his soul on the paper and then destroyed it! After that encounter, we quickly moved along.

Later, our crew went to the beach. I took a Polaroid picture of a beautiful girl sunning (this time, I did it right). She showed it to her friends, who were amazed. My crewmembers ended up using all my film taking pictures of the girls and making dates. The Polaroid camera had just been launched into the market, and people had never seen anything like it, especially in a place such as Brazil.

On one of my trips, I landed in Thule, Greenland. One evening, after attending a party, I got tired and began walking back to the barracks. Suddenly, I looked up and saw a polar bear near my building. I ran back to the party, terrified. Everyone grabbed their guns and went out to search for the bear. All we found were his tracks.

They took good care of me because the Army personnel had been there a year, and we flew their replacements there. The ones being replaced were excited to go home. If I got injured, they would have to wait for another plane because the plane couldn't leave without a navigator.

While I enjoyed all of the exciting places I was able to explore, I was getting tired of flying two weeks out of every four and began to long for a nine-to-five desk job that would allow me to spend more time with my family. Muriel and I wanted to find a way to return to Hawaii, so I began to craft a plan to make it happen. I went to Gunter AFB, Alabama for six months to attend Staff Officer School. Once I completed the course, I would be qualified for three jobs: navigator, squadron commander, and staff officer. My chances of getting back to Hawaii increased exponentially with each new job I became qualified for. My goal was still to secure a staff job that would require only one flight a month.

In 1963, I qualified for Operation Bootstrap, an eight-month program for officers to complete their bachelor's degree in education, sponsored by the GI Bill. I attended Omaha University in Nebraska with all expenses paid and completed my college education with a bachelor's in education. The degree would enhance my promotion to captain and allow me to teach in the Air Force as well as teach K-12 schools when I eventually retired from the Air Force. I was elated to finally get my degree after taking classes at night or by correspondence for so many years.

One day, after I returned to my quarters from class, I saw everyone watching the television and crying. I asked, "What happened?" They said, "President Kennedy was assassinated." As I joined them watching the television, I started to cry too. He was a Catholic like me, and he was the first president to state publicly that segregation was morally wrong. We were all fond of him and Jackie. He was one of our best presidents.

President Kennedy died on November 22, 1963, a date that many Americans will never forget.

After Lyndon Johnson was sworn in as president, he got a bill passed fulfilling President Kennedy's legacy to pass major civil rights legislation. That same year, the Rev. Martin Luther King Jr. gave his famous "I Have a Dream" speech. Muriel and I just happened to be in Washington visiting family when Dr. King made the speech. I remember being inspired and excited by his powerful vision.

There was a lot of change underway culturally in our country. The Beatles left England and arrived in New York on February 7, 1964, to start their first US tour. They were an instant hit in America! Their music was fresh and original and well-received by their young fans (myself among them).

So many of us were inspired by Muhammad Ali's great career as a boxer. I can still remember his braggadocios catchphrases such as "Float like a butterfly, sting like a bee" and "I'm the greatest," and his famous, cleverly named fights such as "Rumble in the Jungle" and the "Thrilla in Manila." We had never seen a black man with such confidence and swagger who wasn't afraid to put everything on the line—and then deliver again and again. Ali decided to be the best boxer in the world, and he was.

I met Muhammad Ali once in Hawaii. He was attending an Alpha Phi Alpha fraternity dinner dance. An elderly female fan was trying to meet him as he was leaving. I said, "Champ, that old lady is trying to catch up to meet you!" He stopped and waited for her to catch up with his group and greeted her. Afterward, he shook my hand to thank me for my help. I was glad for the chance to meet him because he was one of my role models.

THAILAND

In 1965, I received a one-year remote assignment to the 35th TAC Group at Don Muang AFB, Thailand, as a staff officer. This was a combat assignment, so my family could not go with me. Muriel decided to spend the year in Austin for a long visit with her family.

One of my responsibilities was to handle the distribution of top-secret documents for all military units in Thailand. I had two military guards with me at all times. My guards and I would go to the US Embassy in Bangkok where I would sign for the documents and then carry them back to my office and read all of them. I would then brief the group commander and distribute key documents to the commanders at every base in Thailand. My boss, General Barnick, told me he only wanted to be briefed on things he had to know. It was my job to know everything relevant to our mission and also to brief him on what I thought might happen in the future based on current intelligence.

I had a dedicated plane assigned to me to make the rounds to the various military bases in Thailand. The code signal was "Captain Jones desires the base commander to meet his plane." They would meet me in my plane, engines running, sign a receipt for their documents, and then I would be flown to the next base.

The Thai Secret Service informed me that the word on the street was that there was a $10,000 bounty for me to be captured alive because of the intelligence value of my knowledge. My guards and I were armed with pistols, rifles, and hidden knives. I had undergone special self-defense training to prepare for this assignment. My guards and I practiced "staying alive" training daily. This assignment was very scary and stressful, but I thought, *I only have to survive today. Tomorrow is another day. I will manage one day at a time*, and that got me through.

At night, I slept poorly, hyper-aware of every sound in the room. The slightest noise would make me wake up fully alert and draw my pistol from under my pillow, ready to deal with any problem. I was young and cocky and felt I was trained to handle any situation I encountered, but the stressful environment was affecting my health. I dropped thirty pounds and had to report for a medical checkup. The doctors recommended immediate reassignment to a less stressful job and kept me in bed for a few weeks.

After that, I was assigned as Chief of Air Force Security Forces in Thailand. This job was like being the chief of police in an American city, only for the entirety of all the US Air Force personnel in all of Thailand! My health improved quickly, and I spent the remaining months of my assignment in good condition.

One day, the Thai Secret Service informed me that the Thai Communists were planning to destroy our base. I briefed the commander that I was going to call headquarters in Washington, DC to hire two Thai army companies of one hundred soldiers each to be placed under my command that day to secure the base. He okayed my plan.

Lieutenant Boon, who spoke English, was the Thai liaison officer in command of the two Thai squadrons of infantrymen, second in command to me. The Thai troops under our command were elite units, specially trained and fully armed. As we were forewarned, the Thai Communists did attack the base, striking late one night. Lieutenant Boon was ready. His infantry units allowed them to penetrate the base as part of a trap he had set for them. When they were completely surrounded, the Thai infantry opened fire and annihilated the Thai Communists. In Thailand, they operated by different rules—surrender was not an option. Lieutenant Boon and I became great friends during my tour of duty.

I had so many adventures in Thailand! Once I was attacked by a king cobra snake in Bangkok. I was walking to my office just as the sun was rising. It was cloudy, branches were on the ground from the storm the night before, and visibility was poor. Suddenly, I stopped and went on full danger alert. Up ahead, one of the branches moved! The snake slithered toward me. I started backing up, keeping my eyes on the snake at all times, and looking for a sturdy branch to fight with. When I found a good one, I stood my ground, waiting for the snake to come close enough for me to attack it but not close enough for it to strike me.

"Come on! Come and get this stick, you stupid snake!" I taunted. "I'm gonna beat the #@!& out of you!" When it came within striking distance, I hit it repeatedly with all my might until my arms were too tired to swing. When I stopped, I realized it was dead as a doornail.

Suddenly I remembered that cobras travel in pairs. There was a female snake out there that would likely attack me if it found me anywhere near her dead mate. So, I went to my office and had my staff go out and kill the female snake. I told them to form a line, pistols ready, and walk slowly into the woods. I told them not to come back until they had done it. Well, they located and killed the female snake, which was much smaller.

The next day, I bought a pet mongoose in the Thai village. Mongooses are notorious snake-killers. I fed it carrots and kept it sitting on my shoulder. I named it Ricky.

In our apartment in Bangkok, the toilets were just a hole in the ground in a room. When I had to go, I would open the bathroom door and toss Ricky in. If there was a snake in there, I knew Ricky would kill it. Ricky slept on my bed all night. When I left Thailand, I gave Ricky to a friend.

Living in a foreign country, it was not unusual to get homesick around the holidays. One Thanksgiving, my colleagues were wishing they could have a traditional American Thanksgiving dinner. I declared that I could cook one. I worked out a plan to order everything we needed from America. I would be the head cook, and we would all split the cost. We asked one of our friends who had a large home to host the dinner and invited our military Thai friends and their families to join us.

When Thanksgiving Day arrived, our Thai friends' wives were watching closely as I prepared the turkey. They had never seen a turkey! I rubbed spices all over the bird and stuffed it with stuffing. They said, "Maa, mi dee!" That's Thai for "That's not going to be good." I said, "Dee moc moc"—"It will be very good!"

I put the turkey in the oven, and in a few hours, a mouthwatering aroma began to waft throughout the house. The wives kept trying to peek in the oven, but I said they would have to wait until it was done. When I took the turkey out of the oven and put it on the table with mashed potatoes and gravy, green beans, corn on the cob, salad, and pies, the Thai wives were surprised. They asked how I'd learned how to cook, and I told them my mother taught me. We had a wonderful dinner.

While stationed in Bangkok, my crew and I found we often had time on our hands. To keep ourselves occupied and to build trust with our local hosts, we adopted a local orphanage. We would play with the kids, take them out for ice cream, and perform needed repairs at the orphanage. Being with the kids was a way to ease our loneliness and longing for our own families back at home.

Despite these moments of levity, the job was still perilous. One morning at about 3 a.m., just as I was getting in my military staff car, I heard a noise and immediately called my two guards to join me. There were some Thai nationals carrying cans approaching the back of the military officers' quarters. We arrested them when we smelled gasoline. They were planning to burn down the building! We couldn't believe they were able to get that close to our building without being stopped. The building should have been guarded 24/7. We alerted the proper military authorities to investigate the matter and left, albeit shaken.

One day, I was buying two white ceramic elephants to bring back home and climbed into the back of the pickup truck to hold them and keep them from bumping into each other. Nothing happened, but when I arrived back at the base, it occurred to me that I could have been shot by a sniper. It was easy to get overly relaxed and do stupid things that were unsafe. After that, I tried to stay safe and alert at all times.

In addition to my desk duties, I flew once a month to maintain my navigation skills and qualify for combat flying pay. Once we were flying at night in a storm and my radar image cut out for a few minutes due to the weather. I tried to get it working again while praying like mad that we didn't get into trouble. Just as my radar came back on, I saw something that scared the hell out of me.

"Mountain! Mountain! Climb! Turn right! Turn right!" I shouted. We were about to crash into the face of a mountain. The pilots sprang into action. They pulled back on the controls, turning right as fast and as hard as they could. I shut my eyes, truly believing at that moment that we were going to make contact. There simply wasn't enough time to avoid hitting it. Suddenly, an ugly crunching sound shook the plane— the sound of the craft cutting off the very tops of the trees on the mountain.

I soon discovered that we had been blown way off course from the high winds of the storm. It was night, so no one could see in the dark, and the plane was tossing and turning in the storm. I was so rattled, I lit a cigar to calm myself. We had somehow avoided the mountain and flew out of the storm safely, and I said a prayer thanking the Lord for saving us.

Now that we were out of the bad weather, the night was clear and bright with a full moon. I stood between the pilots smoking my cigar like nothing had happened. The commander said, "How could you have possibly known we were blown so far off course into the path of a mountain in the dark of night?" I took a puff and said what had become my signature line, "Didn't they tell you I'm damn good?"

I couldn't tell them how frightened I had been or that I believed God had saved us. They would have teased me to no end and called me Father Jones. But in my heart, I knew with great certainty that we had been saved. I remember praying, "I thank you, my Lord. You saved our lives. I will spend the rest of my life in your service."

When we landed, bits of wood from the decapitated trees were stuck on the bottom of the plane. The ground crew said it was a miracle! I agreed. I believed that the hand of God allowed our survival and would never be convinced otherwise.

One of the most interesting parts of my time in Thailand was learning customs and practices different from our culture. I was surprised to learn that Lieutenant Boon had four wives. "One wife is not enough," he explained. "If you have two wives, they will fight each other. If you have three, two will gang up on the third. But if you have four, you will have two pairs and peace in the house."

Lieutenant Boon said his religion allowed him four wives. I told him my Catholic faith teaches that we may marry only one wife and you and she become one flesh loving each other while loving God the creator first of all. If it is God's will that you have children, then you are to love them as a gift from God. We had many interesting discussions about our different beliefs.

Once, Lieutenant Boon invited me to have a bowl of chicken and vegetable soup from a street vendor. It cost only a nickel in Thai money. It was very spicy, steaming-hot, and delicious. He told me he liked the drinks in my officers' club because he claimed the liquor was better. I thought nothing of this remark until I visited his club one evening and had a few drinks. The next day, my hangover was so painful, I thought I would die—and I wanted to! I never drank at his club again.

One day Lieutenant Boon invited me to visit his family's store. He asked me if I had any ideas on how to improve the operation to attract more Americans. I noticed an old-fashioned bronze chess set in the back of the store. I loved to play chess and suggested they update the design and put it in the window to attract customers. He took my advice and later told me they had sold like hotcakes! Boon's father made me accept a golden ring with a golden sapphire stone. Boon said they made so much money from my ideas I had to accept the ring or his father would lose face. I still wear it today.

When my tour of duty was up in Thailand at the end of the year, I said goodbye to all my friends, including Lieutenant Boon. We both knew that we had experienced something special by reaching out across our respective cultures to get to know one another at a more profound level. I would be forever grateful to have had the opportunity to immerse so fully into another culture that was so different from my own. I bought new clothes and was ready to go home. I was lean, fit, and athletic and had lost quite a bit of weight.

When my flight touched down in Texas, I got off the plane and literally walked right past Muriel and the kids. I watched them looking for me, still waiting for me to exit the plane. When the last passenger got off, they finally turned and saw me, the only person standing there looking at them.

Muriel gasped and said, "What happened to you?!" I was thirty pounds lighter, and my face was very thin. I was healthy returning from the combat arena, but jumpy and high-strung from living in a constant state of alertness and feeling under threat at all times. I started to cry, I had missed them so much. My time as a military intelligence officer had been challenging, exhilarating, and extremely intense. I had experienced situations where I didn't think I would make it back. Hugging my family, I felt glad to finally be home and looked forward to transitioning back to a normal life.

PARADISE, REVISITED

The Air Force personnel officer called me a week after I joined my family in Texas and informed me that a squadron commander in Hawaii had died suddenly, leaving an urgent vacancy. I immediately said, "I'll take it!" It was a sad occasion, but once again I was at the right place at the right time. The earlier time I had invested to qualify for a squadron commander assignment had paid off.

And so, at long last, in 1966, we returned to Hawaii. We were overjoyed to be returning to our island paradise. One of the very best things about being stationed in Hawaii was living with my family full-time. I had been gone for so long and Muriel had carried a heavy load, as military wives often do, keeping the household together and raising three kids under the age of nine. She had to be mother and father to the kids with me gone, paying the bills, doing the laundry and shopping, preparing meals, cleaning the house, keeping track of the kids' schoolwork, and taking care of the millions of tasks that come with running a household. On top of it all, she worried incessantly for my safety. The stress that I had felt in Vietnam and Thailand was echoed in Muriel's life as she wondered if I would make it back alive. She was exhausted. And on top of that, she was teaching school to help make ends meet. She had a full-time helper at home, but it was still an immense emotional burden.

I loved spending time with the kids! They had grown so much, and it was fun getting to know them again. Sometimes I would get them going by saying, "Hey!"

"What?" they'd ask.

"Let's go for a ride!" I'd reply, and I would run as fast as I could to the car. Angie and Al Jr. would run and jump in the car, squealing all the way. Kim always brought up the rear as she yelled, "Wait for me!" The big kids would put Kim in the middle, and away we would go with the top down in my convertible Alfa Romeo to get some ice cream. I cringe to think that there were no seatbelts back then, and the kids were literally just bouncing around in the back seat with Angie and Al holding Kim down!

Spending time with the kids out of the house was a joy to me—I love kids and I loved fatherhood—but it was also a way to give Muriel some quiet time to herself, something that had been sadly lacking in her life while she carried the weight of our family on her young shoulders. I also made arrangements for Muriel and me to spend time together, hiring babysitters to watch the kids.

We loved taking the kids to outdoor concerts at the Honolulu Zoo or to the beach in Waikiki. We would arrive early to walk around to see the animals. While the band was playing, we would have a picnic on the grass. On the beach, we flew kites and watched the kite fights, where the kite fighters would try to cut other kite strings with their own kite tails, which were covered with glued-on bits of glass. We were mesmerized watching their clever attacks and counter-attacks up in the sky.

Of course, when I wasn't with my family, I was working, and my new assignment came with a significant increase in responsibility. As commander of the supply squadron on Hickam Air Force Base, I would be responsible for three hundred airmen and two hundred civilian employees. The airmen were all assigned to top-ranking master sergeants, senior master sergeants, and chief master sergeants, and the civilians were assigned to supervisors. All these top-ranking sergeants and supervisors reported directly to me. They were all highly qualified and reported any problems concerning morale and living conditions to me that they could not solve.

I'll never forget the first time I reported to Lieutenant Colonel Stemme, the wing chief of supply, my new boss. He was tall and athletic-looking and had a businesslike demeanor.

"You are black," he declared flatly, with no preamble.

"Yes, sir. I've been black all my life," I replied.

It was clear from the get-go that Lieutenant Colonel Stemme did not think I would be effective in this new command. I told him I was trained and very qualified for the job. I added, perhaps unwisely, that he actually did not have the authority to change my assignment because I was black. I told him that the only way he could reassign me would be if he found me incompetent, and since I had not yet begun the job, that would be a premature conclusion. He laughed and said, "I like your spunk! Good luck on the job."

In fairness, I knew that Lieutenant Colonel Stemme's concerns came from his lack of firsthand experience with black officers in general. I also knew that the men I would be leading would have a similar reaction and prepared carefully for my first meeting with my supply squadron. I had the men assemble at the base theater, the only space large enough to hold a group of three hundred men. I entered from the back of the theater, knowing that word had already spread that they would be led by a black officer. The first sergeant called, "Attention!" And everyone stood while I walked down the center aisle to the stage. I wanted them to get a good look at me.

When I arrived at the front of the room, I turned to the men, paused, and issued my first command: "At ease!" The men all sat down. I began by stating, emphatically, that I wanted our squadron to be the best squadron on base. I went on to indicate that I had a particular concern about the airmen's living quarters. The men in my squadron were assigned five to an apartment. I had already inspected a few of these apartments, and they were sadly lacking in creature comforts.

I said, "When I come home from a long day at work, I come home to a house with nice furniture to relax on and a color television to enjoy. And so should you." I told them that my goal was for each of their apartments to have good furniture and a color TV. All three hundred men gave me a standing ovation!

I had previously worked out that I could upgrade the squadron living quarters' furniture from Air Force inventory, at no incremental cost to the men, under the morale and recreation regulations. I told the men their new furniture would be free of charge and it would be delivered within the next three months. I got another standing ovation!

I said, "I also want to see a color TV in your apartments in a month, but you will have to pay for it." I told them they could get a cash advance right away from the first sergeant if they were willing to make a small repayment each month. Splitting the cost amongst five roommates would make this expense minimal for all. The television would be Air Force property and remain in the apartment. Any new person assigned to the room would pay a monthly fee too. That money would return to the squadron fund to help pay for additional new televisions, when needed. Another standing ovation!

I told the men that I would be inspecting their apartments once a month. The residents of the best-kept apartment in the squadron would receive a three-day pass and a bottle of whiskey. Another standing ovation! They liked my goals.

Finally, I told everyone my door was open if anyone had a problem.

Within six months, the morale in the supply squadron was sky-high, and our squadron scored the highest among the male squadrons on the base. (Incidentally, the only squadron better than ours was an all-female squadron!) The wing director of materiel, a general, came by to see for himself what had lifted my squadron morale so high, so other squadrons could follow our example. I told him I would be happy to brief the other squadron commanders on the regulations dealing with the morale and recreation of their men. I shared my belief that a happy airman was a productive airman. He was impressed and made a point of congratulating my boss, Lieutenant Colonel Stemme, for having the best squadron and squadron commander on the base. In the end, Lieutenant Colonel Stemme was forced to concede my effectiveness as a commander, even though I was black and my men were white. Race had nothing to do with being a good commander. My success came from my concern for the morale of my men and knowledge of Air Force regulations.

As commander, I was also responsible for two hundred civilians who were assigned to the supply squadron. Civilians were assigned to supervisors. My job was to meet with the supervisors and top sergeants once a month to discuss any matters from the wing chief of supply or wing director of materiel.

The wing chief of supply (my immediate supervisor) called me into his office one day asking me to fire a civilian employee. I made an investigation and found out that according to our regulations, the civilian employee's behavior warranted a written reprimand or other possible actions short of dismissal. I could have prepared a false report that would have gotten the civilian fired in compliance with the wing chief's wishes. I decided to turn in the accurate report and suffer the supply chief's ire. I never regretted my decision.

After a few years as squadron commander, I was promoted to wing chief of administration when the prior chief rotated back to the mainland. I was actually following a higher ranked officer into this role, but the wing commander had heard of my work as squadron commander, I had completed the requisite staff school training with high scores and he wanted me on his team. As wing chief of administration, I was responsible for ensuring the orders of the wing commander of the entire base were executed by the units on the base. These units were commanded by full colonels. I loved this role because it allowed me to use the full range of the abilities I had built in my time in service. The wing commander would share his vision for a particular initiative and it was my responsibility to translate his vision into a plan and ensure it was executed. I was at the peak of my career.

My new responsibilities also included acting as base mortuary officer, a role that required sensitivity and finesse. The wing commander had been dissatisfied with the work of the prior occupant of this job and believed I was better suited for the job. When a military person died, my job was to contact the next of kin to make arrangements for the funeral. Mr. Bradin was the mortician at the military mortuary. He was a slender man who wore glasses and was very efficient at his job. As the base mortuary officer, I was his boss. He invited me to visit and make an inspection of the mortuary. I suspected that he would try to shock me with a dead body, so I was ready.

As I toured the facility, I saw on one of the tables the naked dead body of a beautiful blonde woman. I approached the corpse and checked her arm to see if they had started embalming her yet. At that point, Mr. Bradin realized I had seen dead bodies before and I knew my job. I had to chuckle, thinking of how the cleaning job I'd held as a boy in a mortuary had prepared me for this day.

One day, one of our retired generals died while surfing. I visited his gorgeous wife, who looked like a model, to see if she wanted to use the military mortuary or a civilian mortuary. She opted for the latter. I offered to drive her, so we rode in my Alfa Romeo with the top down.

When we arrived at the civilian mortuary, the mortician explained all the different plans. She asked, "What is your cheapest plan?"

"I can cremate him and put the ashes in a cigar box," he said.

I was a bit taken aback when she responded, "Good. I'll take that plan." I was thinking of all the generals in Washington who would make the trip to pay their respects and was anxious that her husband be appropriately honored. For the funeral, I ended up putting the box on a stand and covering it all with a profusion of exquisite flower leis. The display looked just fine. I had a staff car meet each visiting general and be at his beck and call until he left. Everything went very well. After the reception, the general's wife explained that her husband had told her that he did not want her to spend a lot of money on his funeral. She had certainly honored his wishes.

One day, a woman called me about burying a child. When I went by her house to meet with her, I saw she was pregnant. I wrote down her request for a tiny casket and the specifications for the arrangements she wanted. I glanced around, thinking the deceased child must be in one of the bedrooms, but then she disclosed that she was still carrying the child, but that it had died. She was waiting for her body to reject it. She said she would call me when the baby was ready to be picked up. I agreed and left her home sorrowful and subdued. It was one of the saddest conversations I've ever had.

One of my men died while riding his motorcycle. I had repeatedly reprimanded this young man for riding without a helmet, and sure enough, he was not wearing one in the accident that killed him. At his funeral, his mother asked me if we could have helped her son. Couldn't we have made him wear his helmet? I gave her a copy of the papers showing that I had counseled him, repeatedly, on the topic. I had even gone so far as to punish him with the removal of a stripe and a pay reduction due to his disobedience of the order to ride with a helmet on. None of these actions mattered in the end, because only he could choose to ensure his own safety.

One of the advantages of a career in the Air Force was that I was always learning new skills and deepening my expertise. In 1962, I was sent to survival school in Seattle for a month. We learned how to survive without assistance if we were ever shot down behind enemy lines.

For the final exam, they dropped us in teams of five into a forested area. Each person was given a potato, an onion, a canteen with a cup, and a knife. We were also given one rabbit. Our mission was to trap game and survive for a week without getting caught.

We set traps but our skills were not adequate to catch enough food for a week. When we got hungry in earnest, we killed the rabbit. I divided the meat into five parts and gave each person their share. I asked if anyone wanted the heart, liver, gizzard, and stomach. No one wanted it, so I took the rabbit innards and put them into my canteen cup with a little water and some of my potato and onion. I had brought along a small quantity of garlic, pepper, and salt, which I proceeded to add to the mixture. As my concoction cooked, it emitted a mouthwatering aroma. When the digested grasses in the rabbit's stomach cooked, they tasted like cooked spinach. It was delicious! Everyone wanted a taste. Sometimes it is the smallest items that make the biggest difference in a meal.

After I had my rabbit stew for dinner, I cut my portion of the meat into thin slices to dry out on rocks next to the fire into a jerky that would last until we were picked up. We were having so much fun on our adventure that we hid when the helicopter flew over our area. We lasted for three extra days before they found us and picked us up. We knew that in an emergency, we could have spelled out "SOS" on the ground, and a helicopter would have picked us up immediately, but the wilderness training was still extremely useful.

Phase two of our survival school training started with a simulation of being captured to gauge how much harassment we could stand. When we were captured, they put a hood over our heads, and from that point on, we could not see what was happening. We were taken to a mock prison and put into jail cells, where we had to stand at attention for an extended period of time without leaning against the wall. I whiled away the hours by saying the rosary in my mind. Surprisingly, I found I could actually fall into a light sleep in that standing position. We were badgered and questioned repeatedly through the night and were only permitted to provide our name, rank, and serial number. We could say the words "academic situation" at any time, and we would be taken out and returned to the classroom immediately.

I found myself wanting to understand my own limitations and wanting to see how far I could go before I could not take any more. I got all the way to the point where they put me in a coffin and nailed down the top. I was petrified. I remember saying the rosary over and over until they took me out. Even though, intellectually, I understood it was just a simulation, I was thoroughly traumatized and sweating heavily.

After a break, they prepared to do it again. I knew I couldn't go through that ordeal again and said, "Academic situation!" Only a few of my classmates had made it to the coffin test. And no one chose to repeat the coffin exercise a second time.

THE PHILIPPINES

In 1968, I was assigned to the 29th Tactical Airlift Squadron at Clark AFB, the Philippines as Squadron Administration Officer. I worked for the squadron commander and was responsible for checking all reports that were to be mailed to higher headquarters in accordance with Air Force regulations. All complaints came to my office, and I decided the action to be taken or forwarded the issue to the commander's office if appropriate. This was a great assignment because my family could move with me, and I would only be flying once a month.

We lived like kings in the Philippines, given the strength of the dollar versus the Filipino peso then. We hired a full-time cook, Cindy, to prepare meals for our family; Nora, to do household chores; and Roger, to take care of the yardwork. All three of them helped watch the kids, and they felt like an extension of our family. Cindy would meet me at the door when I came home each evening with a drink in hand as was their custom. Muriel hired two other women for sewing and anything else she needed. Wages for domestic staff seemed very low compared to the cost in America, but afforded a good standard of living in the Filipino economy. We were providing locals with good jobs. Our kids attended the American schools and Muriel secured a teaching position right on the military base. Life was good!

At Clark AFB, I had the opportunity to work under the command of Wing Commander General Benjamin O. Davis Jr. He was a legend, as the first African American general in the US Air Force, just as his father before him, Benjamin O. Davis Sr., was the first African American general in the US Army. General Davis Jr. had commanded the Tuskegee Airmen during World War II, the storied group of fighter pilots who collectively were awarded ninety-five Distinguished Flying Crosses and 744 Air Medals while serving in Italy and North Africa. I was proud to be under General Davis Jr.'s command and to meet someone I admired greatly. I think he appreciated the young black officers, such as myself, who were moving through the doors opened by his WWII flyers. We were his legacy.

Most of my time in the Philippines was spent doing paperwork—managing personnel records, creating and publishing squadron regulations, and editing the reports prepared by staff officers for the squadron commander's signature. My squadron commander's aversion to desk work was a godsend to me. My schedule at Clark AFB was, frankly, quite wonderful—flying in combat only once a month and working five days a week with weekends off. This schedule allowed me to have some semblance of a normal family life. I was also able to complete several college courses by mail during this assignment, as part of my plan to prepare myself for a career as a teacher after I retired from the military.

On one occasion, I flew with my squadron commander from Clark AFB to Vietnam. We were there for two weeks. This commander had a bad habit of flying directly into areas that were not assigned where there was active fighting. As we flew near a war zone, we encountered enemy fire and flack that could have easily downed our aircraft. I promised myself that if I made it back to Clark, I would never fly with him again. I always stood willing to do my duty, but no one needs to go into harm's way just for the thrill of it.

When we returned to Clark, the commander told me he would not be inviting me to fly with him again because our office paperwork was piled high on our desks. He told me I had to stay and take care of both his paperwork and mine. I just smiled and said, "Yes, sir."

RETIREMENT

The year 1968 was one of great turmoil in the United States. First, Martin Luther King Jr. was killed in April, and two months later, Bobby Kennedy was assassinated. The nation was still reeling from President Kennedy's death a few years earlier. It was a sad time for our country to lose three great leaders who had such a positive impact on our nation and the world.

The year 1969 was also momentous. Neil Armstrong and Buzz Aldrin walked on the moon on July 20. We were in a race with Russia and we got there first! Now, when I look up at the moon, I see it not just as an astronomical body in the sky but a place humans can go to. It is only a matter of time before we will travel routinely in outer space.

Unfortunately, 1969 was not a great year for my career. The war in Vietnam had become exceedingly unpopular and our country was in generational turmoil. Richard Nixon had been elected president in 1968 and began to implement a policy of "Vietnamization," shifting combat responsibility to South Vietnam and drawing down American troops in Vietnam, as he had promised during his campaign. This reduction in force was ordered for those stationed in Vietnam. I was still at Clark AFB in the Philippines when I received my orders discharging me in 1970. I was temporarily sent to California with my family, the closest US soil, to carry out the formal separation. As part of the separation, the military offered me the opportunity to be relocated anywhere in the world I chose. Muriel and I knew we wanted to go back to Hawaii.

Most enlisted service members, especially those who had been drafted, were very happy to be discharged from the military and repatriated to the US. The situation for career military officers was altogether different. When we joined the military, we were promised full retirement after twenty years of service, and many of us had intended to serve out all twenty years. When the military executed its cutbacks, it threw a monkey wrench into many of our plans. Many of us felt betrayed and cheated.

To make matters worse, I had recently been notified by personnel that I was to be promoted to major within the next several months. I had been eagerly awaiting orders of promotion when I suddenly and unexpectedly received orders for forced separation instead. I was essentially being kicked out of the Air Force by an executive order of the president. Ironically, if I had received my orders for promotion to major just a few months earlier, I would not have been discharged at all because, as field-grade officers, majors were not included in the mandatory discharge action.

My peers and I came together before the personnel officer to discuss our problem. He told the group of three hundred officers, both white and black, that he had no choice but to obey the president's order. For those of us who were set on retiring after twenty years of service, we could write a letter requesting reenlistment to serve out the remainder of our tenure. Due to budget constraints, the highest rank we would be permitted to reenlist at would be that of staff sergeant, which, in my case, was a *huge* demotion. If I did serve out the remaining two years at that lower rank, at the end of that period, I would automatically retire at the rank of major.

What a choice! I felt angry and betrayed by the commander in chief. I had served my country so loyally for so long, I could scarcely believe that this was happening. It is hard to convey the humiliation of serving at a rank well below that which you have earned at great risk to life and limb. It wasn't just the cut in pay. It was the loss of prestige and stature within a culture that is all about rank. The whole hierarchical military system is based on outward symbols and insignia that convey exactly what any given individual has accomplished in their career. When we were in uniform, we literally wore our status on our sleeve. How could I be expected to present myself as having achieved less than I had? How could I face people who knew me? If I reenlisted, I would be working on Hickam Air Force Base and was bound to run into people I knew. They would wonder what I had done to get demoted down to staff sergeant.

In a show of appreciation of our service, the military was offering a lump-sum payment of $15,000 to exiting officers. This felt like a king's ransom at the time, and many of my colleagues were happy to take this sizable payout to launch their post-combat civilian lives. But I was stubborn. I knew what I had earned, and I knew that full retirement pay at the rank of major, medical care for myself and my family, privileges shopping on base, and access to air travel—for the rest of my life—were worth more. A lot more.

I realized that the best decision for me and my family was to reenlist at the lower rank and serve out my remaining two years to retirement. And so, I swallowed my pride and sent a letter to the department of the Air Force requesting reenlistment. I went from captain to staff sergeant with the stroke of a pen; a bitter pill to swallow, even without the large reduction in pay. I was assured that I would retire at the rank of major, so I knew that my sacrifice would be worthwhile. I could do it.

To add insult to injury, a few months later I was contacted by the chief of personnel and notified that I had been awarded the Distinguished Flying Cross (DCF), the highest honor a flyer can receive for outstanding service in the Air Force, as well as two Air Medals (I had previously received two others). The DFC was for my performance as a staff master navigator in charge of dropping Army paratroopers from three aircraft formations on the special top-secret mission in Korea at a very dangerous drop zone. One Air Medal was for outstanding performance of duty in saving our plane from crashing into a mountain in a hazardous area at night and in a violent storm. The other medal was in recognition of when our plane was blown off course and I guided the plane in an emergency landing on Iwo Jima.

To receive this recognition was an incredible honor. Typically, when the DFC is awarded, its presentation is accompanied by a full base parade. What should have been the pinnacle of my career was irreparably tarnished due to the circumstances I found myself in.

Imagining the humiliation of receiving this honor at a full base parade in the uniform of a staff sergeant, I was filled with mortification and anger. I stiffly told the chief of personnel, "Here is what we are going do. I will receive the medals in full uniform at the rank of major in the base commander's office after I retire. I do not want the parade."

When the Air Force moved us back to Hawaii, Muriel began teaching at Waipahu Intermediate School. By then, Angie was thirteen years old, Al was twelve, and Kim was eight. Muriel and I had decided that the most important investment we needed to make was in our children's education. The public schools in Hawaii at that time were below par, so we sent the children to private schools; Angie to Punahou School and Al Jr. and Kim to Our Lady of Good Counsel, the school affiliated with the parish I had helped build. We wanted our children to have a good grounding in our Catholic faith and be prepared to go on to college. We also wanted our kids to feel comfortable in any academic or social setting. We were raising citizens of the world.

Hawaii is an expensive place to live in. Everything needs to be shipped into the island: food, fuel, building materials, everything. With three kids in private school, our budget was very tight for the next two years, but with Muriel's teacher salary and my lower staff sergeant pay, we managed to pay our bills and make ends meet.

When I first returned to Hickam Air Force Base as a staff sergeant, I was very depressed. I told no one that I was back in Hawaii. I was terrified of running into former colleagues. I was so embarrassed to wear a staff sergeant uniform that I would drive to work in civilian clothes and change in the men's room once I arrived at work. I did this for several months.

Gradually, I began to let go of my anger. After all, being humbled was not the worst thing that could befall a person in the military. I was alive, I had made it through a war, and I had a loving family who brought me joy. I resolved not to let the situation define me and to do the very best job possible in my remaining years of service. I did not feel I had been treated honorably, but I could not let that impact how I conducted myself. I knew the Air Force was helping me as much as they were able, but their hands were tied.

In a nod to my "true" rank, the base commander (my boss) designated me chief of the base Flight Records Office, a job normally assigned to a major. He had read my file and was glad to have me on his staff. I appreciated that the Air Force was trying to meet me halfway.

This job challenged me and allowed me to solve problems at a level commensurate with my true rank and ability.

In my first meeting with the base commander, he told me the office was a mess and he hoped I could improve it. It was all I needed to stop feeling sorry for myself and dig in. He treated me as though I was a major, one of his field-grade officers, and fully expected me to solve the problems within the unit and bring the records office up to the level of an efficient operation. My goal was to make it one of the best in the Air Force.

The base flight records office is responsible for tracking the flight activity of all flying personnel on the base, including the wing commander. This is a critical function because flight records are used to plan for aircraft and other equipment appropriations, to track flight hours associated with promotions and recognition, and to ensure adequate crew rest. In the branch of the military entirely concerned with flight, flight records matter! Each Air Force base had to send an updated report monthly to the Air Force Command Flight Records Office in Washington, DC. The master computer there would evaluate the accuracy of all reports received.

The first thing I did in my new role was survey the department's level of performance. I found the error rate was a whopping 30 percent! That means that 30 percent of the time, our data differed from data at the records office in Washington, DC! The base commander was right—it was a mess!

I had both military and civilian personnel working in the Base Flight Records Office. A woman named Mrs. Nakamura was my next-in-command. She was a slim Japanese woman who had a brisk, businesslike demeanor; she was well-qualified to command the office. Unfortunately, Mrs. Nakamura could not identify the reason for the high error rate. I assessed the entire team and found that they were all well-trained. So, what was causing the problem?

To kick the tires on the system, a week before the flight records report was due to the master computer in Washington, DC, I submitted a flight report to DC to test it for accuracy. I received a reply that showed a 30-percent error rate. I then made the corrections by hand and resubmitted the corrected report to the master computer at the normal report date. The error rate dropped from 30 percent to 2 percent. I had identified a temporary solution to reduce the error rate. Doubling our workload with a dual submission strategy was not a sustainable practice, but it gave me the time I needed to identify the root cause of the problem. My early test also gave me the clue I needed to develop a permanent solution.

My experiment told me that the high error rates had to do with how submitted flight reports were being processed by the master computer in DC. Further investigation revealed a simple explanation. These were still the early days of computing. Crackerjack programmers in Washington, DC were racing to make our computers faster, better, and smarter every day, but the modifications they made to the master computer sometimes required formatting changes in how flight records from around the world were submitted to the centralized hub. Flight offices around the world (like mine) were not being informed of the new formatting requirements in a timely fashion, and therefore, flight data was not always being submitted to Washington in the proper format. Amazingly, we weren't the only ones with this problem—it was impacting all flight records offices around the world! The implications of my discovery were enormous.

I notified the base commander that I had reduced our error rate to 2 percent and was taking action that would reduce the error rate in the entire Air Force. I also informed him that our office would become one of the best record offices in the Air Force. Needless to say, the commander was astonished—and a tad skeptical. He said he had not expected me to produce results so quickly. I was so confident I had cracked the nut on the problem that I proposed the commander allow me to adopt a flexible work plan in which I would train Mrs. Nakamura as my replacement, while I spent additional time volunteering as a teacher at my parish school.

I had loved the challenge of figuring out how to improve performance. Problem-solving had always been my strong suit, and it was just what I needed to get me through the initial humiliation of service at a lower rank. But once I had solved the problem, the job held little interest for me. My eyes were turned toward retirement and my future transition into civilian life. I had resolved to become an educator in the second phase of my professional career. I loved being around kids and, remembering the impact Mrs. Catlett had on me all those years ago, I thought I could make a difference in young lives, too.

The base commander acceded to my requested work schedule, but said I would have to maintain the new high level of performance for the flight records office and that he expected to receive confirmation from Washington, DC regarding the broader impact of my discovery for the Air Force. I felt confident that I could make good on both of these requirements.

I called the chief of the Air Force flight records office in Washington, DC, explained the problem, and proposed implementing a new policy to notify flight records offices around the world of new formatting requirements, with a one week lead time, to ensure reports would be submitted correctly. I also asked the chief if he would be willing to send my commander a letter confirming the performance of our flight records office and the impact of my discovery on the Air Force. I noted that I had a bet with the base commander and needed the letter to win my bet.

One month later, the base commander presented me with a letter of commendation from the chief of the Air Force Flight Records Office for solving a problem that saved the Air Force millions of dollars and improved the efficiency of computer operations worldwide. The letter also validated that we had one of the most efficient records offices in the Air Force.

I finally received orders for retirement in 1972 and was instructed to report to the base commander. I bought a new major's uniform and reported as ordered. My family was invited to attend the ceremony. The base commander presented me with a letter from President Nixon commending my retirement as a major with twenty years of outstanding service and congratulating me for earning the Distinguished Flying Cross and two Air Medals.

My twenty years of military service were over! As a result of my decision to swallow my pride for two years and wear the rank of sergeant, I would receive full retirement pay at the rank of major until the day I died. I would also receive full medical benefits and be able to buy food and clothing at the commissary and base exchanges and take advantage of travel space available anywhere in the world for the rest of my life. I was a young man, only forty-two at the time, so these lifetime benefits would be enormous.

Ultimately, I was pleased with my career. I appreciated the opportunity the Air Force had given me to realize my dream of flying. I had been able to travel the world while serving my country and had made a living that allowed me to support my family. I had acquired many invaluable skills in the Air Force; not just technical skills related to my career as a navigator, but leadership skills that would serve me well for the rest of my life. I had also learned how to solve problems creatively and how to work with all kinds of different people. In the end, I was grateful to the Air Force for allowing me to serve out my twenty-year career and allowing me to retire at the rank I had earned through my service. The military was a tremendous enabler in my life.

Alphonso Beverly Jones and Aloysius Fredroy Jones
(my twin brother), born January 25, 1932

Beverly Jones (father), Mildred Jones (mother),
Aloysius, Beulah (sister) and me, circa 1936

Relay Honors: Mile Relay at National Guard Armory, Mile Relay at Philadelphia
RECORD-BREAKING RELAY at Madison Square Garden.

CROSS COUNTRY TRACK CHAMPIONS
Cardozo's Track Team take top honors: District of Columbia Meet, South Atlantic

Aloysius and me (fourth to the right of the coach)
with the Cardozo High School Track Team

Beulah and me

My appointment as a commissioned officer
(Second Lieutenant) in the US Air Force

Me as a First Lieutenant in the US Air Force (left) and
Aloysius as a Michigan ROTC cadet (right)

Becoming a navigator

Our Wedding, 1956

Cutting our wedding cake with my military saber

My beautiful wife, Muriel

Cruising to Hawaii on *The Lurline*

Our first child, Angela Leilani, born May 15, 1957

Sweet Leilani, heavenly flower

Muriel, Angie and I with our beloved son,
Alphonsus Beverly, born July 23, 1958

Me, Muriel, Al and Angie with little
Kimberly Ann, born September 5, 1962

Left to right: Aloysius, Elizabeth (his wife),
Muriel and me

Out on the town: (left to right) Elizabeth,
Guest, Muriel, me and Aloysius

Serving combat duty in Thailand 1965,
surrounded by my staff

Coming home from Vietnam in 1966

Receiving the Distinguished Flying Cross and Air
Medals at retirement, 1970

The Distinguished Flying Cross Certificate

THE UNITED STATES OF AMERICA

TO ALL WHO SHALL SEE THESE PRESENTS, GREETING:

THIS IS TO CERTIFY THAT
THE PRESIDENT OF THE UNITED STATES OF AMERICA
AUTHORIZED BY EXECUTIVE ORDER, MAY 11, 1942
HAS AWARDED

THE AIR MEDAL
(FIRST THRU THIRD OAK LEAF CLUSTER)

TO

CAPTAIN ALPHONSO B. JONES

FOR
MERITORIOUS ACHIEVEMENT
WHILE PARTICIPATING IN AERIAL FLIGHT

24 December 1968 to 4 May 1970
GIVEN UNDER MY HAND IN THE CITY OF WASHINGTON
THIS   30th   DAY OF   November   19 70

GENERAL, USAF

SECRETARY OF THE AIR FORCE

The Air Medal certificate
(First through Third Oak Leaf Cluster)

BECOMING AN EDUCATOR

As I transitioned from the military into civilian life, Our Lady of Good Counsel Church (OLGC) became central in my life. We had attended the church, located in Pearl City, from those early days I helped to build it, and adopted it as our home parish. When I retired in 1972, I started teaching at the parish K-8 school full-time. Sister Candida, the principal of OLGC School, was very happy to have me on her faculty. Sister Candida, like most of the nuns who ran the school, wore a black and white nun's habit. She was a kind and gentle woman, with a soft, prayerful voice, but a backbone of steel and a determination to deliver the best possible education to the children in her care. It was obvious that she enjoyed her job and took her responsibility very seriously.

The only position that was open at the time I joined the school was third-grade teacher. Sister Candida planned for me to teach math to grades six through eight the following year. I took an enrichment course on elementary school techniques that helped me prepare for teaching the third grade.

What a fun first year I had as an educator! Each morning, I came to work one hour early to open my room to all the first-, second-, and third-grade students whose parents had to drop them off before school. I had a pair of hamsters the kids could play with before school. I went to a hatchery and got chicken eggs that were about to hatch. I put them in an incubator, which I had purchased for my classroom, so that the kids could see them emerge from their shells. This was all part of my hands-on science program. Once the baby chicks hatched, they followed me around the classroom as their "mother" until I made a cage for them. One day, the mother hamster gave birth to a baby hamster, and the next day we had a baby hamster to play with.

These animals became an important part of the classroom experience. The kids were even allowed to take the pets home on the weekends with their parents' permission.

With all the animals available, the little kids were now rushing to school each morning to play with the baby chicks and hamsters. My room was always filled with kids before school, at recess, and after school until they were picked up by their parents. I still look back on fond memories of little kids running into my classroom to play with a pet before school started. The parents were happy their children suddenly seemed to like school so much.

I bonded with the children in other ways, too. One day, a little girl said to me, "I need a hug." She had a great sadness about her, and I wondered if she was having problems at home. I got down on my knees, and she gave me a hug.

Seeing this, of course, *all* the little kids decided they needed a hug too. So, there I was, on my knees, with these little kids giving me hugs every morning. Some wanted to talk about some problems they had. What was I getting myself into by opening my room in the morning? Who knew this would happen?

Sister Candida asked what all these hugs were about. I explained how it had come about. Sister dropped by my room the next morning and saw the kids asking me to kneel down so they could get their hugs. Some of the parents saw them hugging me and were very touched to see the connection forming between us. It is important for kids to have safe, loving adults in their lives.

I started coming to school two hours earlier to set up my classes for the day, so I could be available for one hour just to listen to the children's concerns and stories of their pets and home life.

Sister said, "Don't you mind putting in all those extra hours here?"

"No," I said. "I don't mind at all. I am glad to be here. I read a book about how pets can positively influence the behavior of children. I can see how it is working. I think the parents appreciate it too."

Sister Candida was very happy having me at OLGC. She had always wanted a male teacher on her staff whom kids could relate to.

Once, two kids came to school with dog bites on their hands. I called the child protection office to check out this serious problem and to keep me posted. Apparently, there was a dog in the household that was biting the children. The parents were told they would have to get rid of the dog or their kids would be taken away. The kids got proper medical care. I checked them every day at school to make sure they were okay and that it didn't happen again.

One day, one little girl came in with a very serious problem. She told me that her father had killed her pet cat.

I said, "Oh, I'm so sorry about the accident."

"Noooooo, Mr. Jones. He did it on purpose!" she said.

Sister Candida and I were somewhat skeptical. We checked with the girl's mother, who admitted that it was quite possible that he had done it on purpose. She said that this man was her second husband and not the children's father. Quietly, she then conceded that he did not like her children or their cat. Sometimes life can be really sad for kids.

My classroom was a safe haven for this little girl and her brother. I was like a father to them. They spent time with me in the morning and at recess and after school. Sometimes, when their mother picked them up after school, they would not want to go home.

I remember one day we had to fill in a survey on each kid in our homeroom. There was a place for race. A new teacher asked me for advice. I said, "Put down what the kids tell you."

A kid named Darnell told her he was Spanish. She said, "Darnell, you are black!" He said, "No, I'm Spanish." The teacher said, "I'm going to write black." The next day, Darnell's mother came to school. I saw her walk by my room. She was a beautiful Spanish lady. I heard her chewing out the teacher next door. "I'm Darnell's mother! His father is black! If he wants to say he's Spanish, that's all right! He is Spanish *and* black!"

Another time I filled out the paperwork for a boy who looked Japanese but told me he was white. I wrote down "white." Everything was cool. I got no complaints from Mr. and Mrs. Gaelic, his white father and Japanese mother. In fact, his father gave my son a job in the stock room of his Sears store after Al Jr. graduated from high school.

Living in Hawaii, you are surrounded by literally every skin color and racial combination under the sun. Our islands probably have the greatest percentage of mixed-race people in America—maybe on the planet. This is one of the things I love most about the islands. Because everyone is such a mix of everything, it is difficult to single anyone out for discrimination or persecution. It is impossible to tell from someone's physical appearance what is in their DNA. Not being able to rely on race as a shorthand for stereotyping others forces us to judge them by other factors, like character or accomplishments. I wish all of America could experience the beauty of Hawaii's racially mixed bag.

After my first year of teaching third grade at OLGC, true to her word, Sister Candida assigned me to teach fifth- to eighth-grade math. My youngest daughter, Kim, was one of my students. She didn't seem to mind this strange state of affairs and was delighted to spend additional time with me in our math class. When she raised her hand to ask a question, she just called me "Daddy" as if it were the most natural thing in the world.

Some of the other kids started calling me Daddy too. "Don't try it," I said, putting an end to that experiment.

Sometimes other students teased Kim about my being her math teacher. Once, a student said, "Kim is getting an A in math because you are her father." I said, "No, Kim's getting an A in math because she is a hard worker and good at math."

I told them to pick a homework problem for her to do and called her up to the chalkboard to do it. Kim got it right, and that seemed to satisfy the students. They began working harder too. I provided tutoring for those who needed extra help. Kim was a good student and just seemed to take it in stride that her dad was her math teacher.

One of my jobs at OLGC was to create an athletics program for the school. We started a basketball team and entered the Junior High School Catholic Basketball League. I really lucked out. We had a boy who was tall and a very good player. I guessed that his father had taught him how to play basketball and approached his father to see if he would consider coaching our team. I hit the jackpot! This kid's father coached us into winning the league championship!

A team in California wanted to come to Hawaii and play us. I talked it over with Sister Candida and the school staff. My dream was to organize an exchange trip for their boys to visit Hawaii and for ours to visit California. My vision was that our Hawaii parents would only have to pay for airfare and pocket money for their sons and we would wash cars and ask for donations to help defray that expense.

We arranged the logistics, and soon, the California team arrived in Hawaii. We had the better basketball team, so to keep the score close, I had our coach substitute our less-skilled players.

Later, our boys were very excited to visit Modesto, California for part two of the program. Our youth had never been away from Hawaii, so they were nervous, scared, and thrilled at the same time. I am sure the Californian kids felt the same way coming to Hawaii for the first time.

The day we arrived was a cold one. Our boys were walking around outside, and one of them said, "My feet hurt." The kids were wearing their flip-flops instead of their basketball sneakers. No wonder. After that, they wore their sneakers everywhere.

The California families worked hard to show us a good time. They even had a dance at their school for the Hawaii team. Their girls were quite bold and quite comfortable asking our boys to dance. Our boys were shy at first, but quickly got used to talking to the upfront California girls. They had wonderful stories to tell when we arrived back in Hawaii. We never forgot the hospitality of the host families and the entire school.

I was also one of the coaches for the girls' volleyball team (I was, technically, the school's athletic director). I lucked out again! I found a mother of one of the students who had played volleyball in college and got her to agree to coach the team. Her daughter was highly skilled, and we held our own playing the other teams in the Junior High School Catholic Girl Volleyball League. It was a delightful experience traveling by bus to other schools in Hawaii to play volleyball, and the kids really came out to support the home games.

Having spent so much time away while Al Jr. was growing up, one of my priorities in retirement was to spend more time with my son. He had grown up as a middle child surrounded by women, and I knew he needed a closer relationship with his dad. I wanted to find a good Boy Scout troop for us to participate in together. Al Jr. loved the idea of being a Boy Scout.

I said, "Al, how would you like to go camping on the weekends? We could live in a tent and cook on an open fire."

Al Jr. loved the idea and replied, "Wonderful, Daddy, that would be great!"

I said, "How often do you want to go camping?"

"I don't know, maybe once every two or three months?" he replied.

I suggested, "How about we go every month?"

He responded enthusiastically, "Yeah! Let's go every month!"

I could not find a troop that I liked, so I took a scoutmaster course and started my own troop. Al began calling his friends and telling them that his dad was starting a scout troop and asking if they wanted to join. Many of Al's friends also had fathers in the military who were away from home much of the time. One's father had died in Vietnam.

We started out by earning merit badges related to camping and cooking. I borrowed tents, sleeping bags, and cooking equipment from the Air Force recreational office. The military was truly the gift that kept on giving in my life.

On our first campout, I taught the boys to put up my large tent first and put everyone's personal equipment and camping equipment inside it. Next, they had to put up a large overhead canopy for a cooking tent. After that, the boys could set up their tents and transfer their personal equipment to their tents. My tent was the troop supply tent. I had plenty of room because the Air Force tents were large eight-man tents.

After the boys got the tents up, I divided them into "patrols" of five or six boys each. The boys selected one scout to be the patrol leader. One patrol was in charge of gathering dry wood for the fire, and one was in charge of starting the fire; they dug a hole and lined it with rocks. Another patrol was assigned to prepare the meal and, yet another patrol would get buckets of water for emergencies and cooking.

Each patrol cooked meals for their group. The fire was big enough for all patrols to do so at the same time. Every evening, a different patrol was assigned to cook the scoutmaster's meal. This gave me a chance to taste and critique their cooking. I took notes and gave them feedback on how well they performed their duties.

My youngest daughter, Kim, who was around ten at the time, was always desperate to go camping with us. I tried to explain to her that Boy Scouts was for boys only, but she argued that she could go as my helper. She pleaded with me so much that I finally agreed.

"Only if you don't embarrass me," Al Jr. said. Kim was delighted.

We took Kim on a trial campout, and she generally stayed with me and away from the boys. I had a great time with her because Al Jr. was a trained leader in the troop and spending most of his time with the other boys. Once the boys were trained to run the troop, there actually wasn't much for me to do.

Al Jr. was very happy to be camping with his dad and his friends. Kim learned how to cook on an open fire. We cooked our meals together, and I would point out the stars and share the Hawaiian stories of how the stars were related to their Hawaiian gods. She was the happiest little girl on the planet!

Since I was not only a trained scoutmaster, but also a certified teacher and trained in survival techniques, I was authorized to sign all the merit badges the boys earned. Over time, some of the boys progressed through the ranks of Tenderfoot, Second Class, First Class, Star, Life, and Eagle Scout. My son became the first Life Scout, and a boy named Spanky Ratcliff became our first Eagle Scout. At this point, the boys were able to completely run a campout. I was there only if they needed help or if there was an emergency.

The only other thing I needed were a few additional adults who could be available to help supervise the boys on camping trips. I finally found two fathers and a junior Air Force officer who liked to camp and would alternate attending campouts. One of the parents had a son with an emotional disability. Our youth troop leaders assigned the boy duties they thought he could do, and he fit right into the fabric of our troop. His father was pleased that his son enjoyed scouting and was freely accepted by the other boys. We were now a highly trained troop able to execute camping trips with excellence and consistency.

We participated in many camping events, such as Makahikis, camporees, and other large competitive scouting events from 1971 to 1976. One of our favorite places to camp was Camp Pupukea, located in the mountains on the north shore of Oahu. We also managed to go camping on our own, just for fun, at least twice a month each year.

One campout on the Big Island was unforgettable. We were at the Kilauea Camp site, and one night we woke up to the sound of the Kilauea volcano (one of the largest in the world) spewing lava hundreds of feet into the air! It had been twenty-five years since the last eruption, but it had come alive again. There was no danger because we were seventeen miles away, but at night, it looked like just a few miles.

The boys wanted to hike closer to the spectacle, and so I said, "Let's go!" They got dressed, put on their backpacks, and we were off on an adventure. I knew we would not get far and made sure we were hiking on a trajectory that would keep us safe. After a while, they said, "Mr. Jones, we should go back to camp." They were tired of walking. So, we walked back to camp and everyone went back to bed. They were sound asleep within minutes. Scoutmasters are so sneaky! I knew the only way I could get a bunch of excited scouts to settle down was to take them on a hike.

The next morning, we were sent back home due to safety concerns as the eruptions continued. The scouts couldn't wait to tell everyone about their exciting experience on the big island during the Kilauea eruption. Some of the old Hawaiians started praying to the Hawaiian goddess of fire, Madam Pele (or Tutu Pele in the local language).   With Hawaii being a chain of volcanic islands, eruptions are just part of life.

Once, Muriel and I purchased land on the big island. After a few years, we sold it and invested in stocks instead. Later, the Kilauea volcano erupted and lava flowed down the mountain, crossing the highway and destroying everything in its path, including the land that we had once owned.

They highway actually had to be rerouted because the massive lava flow blocked the old highway. On a trip to the Big Island, I visited the lava site on the highway and saw a group of tourists who were moving to step on the lava to take pictures. I shouted, "Stop! The lava looks solid and cool, but under the top crust is hot lava! If you break through the top thin layer, your foot would instantly be incinerated. You would be crippled for life!" They looked at me in astonishment, but did back away from the seemingly solid lava flow. There were signs warning against approaching the lava, but I guess some people just don't believe they are in danger.

One Easter Eve, my eldest daughter, Angie, and I decided to camp overnight on Diamond Head Mountain, joining many others to share prayers at sunrise Easter morning. We took our sleeping bags and everything we needed for an overnight stay. We studied the stars and joined in the singing until we fell asleep. We got up just before sunrise and joined in the prayers and songs. We then walked down and had a hearty breakfast at a restaurant before going home. What a great outing with my sweet Leilani.

I had so much fun with our kids. We went to the movies, parades, concerts, charity walks (like the "Walk for Mankind"), and, of course, camping. Each child had different interests. Angie loved the stage, and we shared a passion for the ballet and the Hawaii Symphony Orchestra. I had season tickets to all the plays and concerts.

Angie loved books too. We read the entire set of Edgar Rice Burroughs' *Tarzan of the Apes* books together. Later, Al Jr. and Kim joined Angie and me in reading the Tarzan series, too. I told the kids that Mr. Burroughs had lived for a while in Hawaii.

Al Jr. and I connected primarily through camping and sports. Kim shared our love of camping and also had an affinity for reading and riding horses. I am so grateful to have had time and energy to spend with the kids.

One special aspect of living in Hawaii was that my twin brother Aloysius ended up moving to Oahu with his family in 1973. They bought a home with a swimming pool and a guest house on the other side of the island of Oahu, in the town of Kailua. Our families often referred to each other as the "Kailua Joneses" and the "Aiea Joneses." We enjoyed a very special relationship with my brother's family. Our kids grew up celebrating birthdays and holidays together and sometimes we just got together and hung out for no particular occasion. Al's wife, Elizabeth, remodeled their beautiful home to create a bed and breakfast business to earn extra money for their trips to Germany to visit her family. Elizabeth advertised their bed and breakfast in Germany and built an extensive roster of German clients who appreciated staying in a guest house in Hawaii with people who spoke their language.

Once, our two families had a party at Hanauma Bay Beach, an underwater wildlife preserve in Hawaii. The kids snorkeled and swam in the warm waters of the bay, Al Jr. showed off the fruits of his weightlifting, and Muriel walked around with a large lobster trying to scare the kids. The girls danced the hula to the music on the radio—we had a great time. My brother hiked out, with a few of the kids, to a rocky outcropping called "the toilet bowl," a natural, enclosed circular rock formation in the ocean. When a wave crashes in, the hole fills with water, and as the wave goes out, the water drains out of the hole. People jump into the hole when the water is at the high point, and are settled to the bottom of the hole as the wave washes out. When the next wave crashes in they are buoyed forcefully back up to the top of the hole, where they can scramble out. Our kids wanted to try it, but my brother wouldn't let them because the rocks looked sharp, and if you weren't careful, it looked like you might be sucked out of the hole as the water left.

Hanauma Bay was pristine in those days; the beautiful white sand beach was uncrowded, and the bay was full of all manner of colorful marine life. Nowadays there are long lines and tourist buses lined up to visit the bay. Over the years, human traffic has damaged the fragile coral reefs and stressed the marine ecosystem. Today the wildlife preserve is a shadow of what it used to be.

Muriel and I took our kids and my brother's two daughters to see the Jackson Five's "Aloha from Hawaii" concert in 1973. We had great seats near the stage, and midway through the concert, everyone rushed to the front of the stage, including us. Michael Jackson wiped the sweat from his face with a small towel and then threw the towel out into the audience. My niece, Jackie, jumped up and caught it. She was thrilled to have snagged this priceless souvenir!

My brother and his wife had stayed home because they thought the music would be too loud, which it was. "How did you manage with the loud music?" my brother asked me later.

"I wore earplugs!" I replied.

A STAR, A SOLDIER AND A STUDENT

ANGIE

Angie attended Our Lady of Good Counsel Catholic School through fifth grade. Securing a great education for our children was our number one priority. Muriel and I had researched the schools on the island and determined that Punahou School, a local college preparatory academy, was the best option. The school was a financial stretch for us, but we were determined to prepare our children to lead successful lives and were willing to invest whatever it took to make it happen. The school we chose had one particularly noteworthy student, a tall, slim, black kid with an afro who would later play a pivotal role in our country's history.

From the very beginning, Angie loved to perform. She was in *The Singing Nun* in the first grade and played the lead in *Charlie Brown* in the sixth grade. When she started at Punahou School, her skills in singing, dancing, and acting just took off. She played piano, joined the choir, became a fixture in Punahou's dance company, and was cast as the lead in many productions staged by the high school. Leilani was truly gifted; that rare breed of performer who can sing, dance, and act.

Angie also became a fixture on the local theater scene. Her first paid acting role was in *South Pacific* at the Hawaii Theater, and she performed in many plays at Manoa Valley Theater for the Performing Arts, including as lead in *Iolanthe*.

Angie was also an outstanding scholar. She loved learning and did exceptionally well academically. When Angie graduated from Punahou, she was awarded Punahou's Presidential Award for academic excellence and excellence in the performing arts.

As Angie approached her senior year of high school, she resolved to pursue her passion for the performing arts in college. Muriel wanted her to go to college but not to study acting! She saw theater as a hobby or interest, not a career.

It was difficult for Muriel to reconcile Angie's interest in performing with her potential to succeed in any number of more traditional professions. She was an academic superstar and the sky was the limit for how far that could take her. Muriel believed she knew what was best for Angie: getting a four-year college degree that could pave the way to a career that would allow her to support herself.

We saw pursuing an acting career as akin to hoping to play in the NFL—a one-in-a-million moonshot that seemed destined to derail her promising young life. We had worked so hard and invested everything we had in order to give Angie a world-class education—all to provide her with the broadest set of choices in life. It felt like she was throwing her education away on a pipedream. It was galling to us that of all the things our brilliant daughter could do, she was choosing a high-risk career that offered limited opportunities for people of color and was jam-packed with predators. We felt we were protecting Angie from making a bad decision she would regret for the rest of her life.

One day, Angie came to me in tears, saying, "Dad, I want to be an actress, and Mom wants me to be a lawyer!"

I told her, "I will support you, whatever your career choice."

Angie begged, "Talk to Mom."

I had encouraged Angie in her study of music, dance, and theater throughout her life, taking her to the ballet and the symphony orchestra, and attending all of her performances. I wanted Angie to pursue her dreams, but Muriel was immovable in her opposition.

Adding additional pressure to the situation was our family's financial challenges at the time. Even with three kids in private school at the same time, Muriel and I had set aside some modest savings. Unfortunately, we had made an investment that had recently gone south. We simply couldn't afford to send her to the mainland to school. In hindsight, we now know that for a talented, bright young scholar such as Angie, there would have been scholarships and financial aid even back in 1975. But she was our first child to go through the process and these options were not explored.

The long and short of it was that our daughter knew what she wanted and she wanted to perform. She believed in her dream and her own potential as a singer, dancer, actress. It was what she wanted to do. Believing in yourself is the most important gift you can have in life. It is helpful, but not necessary, for those around you also believe. As parents, we can advise, but in the end, our kids must make their own choices. Our only choice is whether or not to support them.

In the end, Angie decided that she would study what she wanted to study and pay for that privilege. As many of her friends at Punahou traveled to the mainland to Ivy League colleges to study more traditional subjects, Angie moved out of the house and put herself through four years at the University of Hawaii studying music theory by working on the Waikiki nightclub circuit. She performed in one campus production of *Oklahoma!* and also in many other productions in the local theater scene.

Attending Angie's plays and giving her a big bouquet of flowers at the end was the highlight of our lives. We could see how committed she was to a career in the performing arts. We gradually began to understand that our job, as parents, was not to protect her from potential failure in her chosen career, but to support her through the inevitable ups and downs she would experience in life, regardless of what profession she chose. Parenting is a journey for us all. There is no instruction manual. This was a lesson we had to learn the hard way.

Angie moved to New York City in 1979 after she graduated from the University of Hawaii to audition for plays, adopting her middle name, Leilani, as her stage name. She lived with a family friend, Jermaine Smith, when she first arrived, but soon began working and was able to move out. She landed her first paid role and an all-important Actors' Equity card (proof of membership in the Actors' Equity Association) in a touring production of *Ain't Misbehavin'* that played across the US and Canada.

Angie also did a lot of regional theater, performing in productions such as *Bloomer Girl* at the Goodspeed Opera House in Connecticut, *Dusky Sally* at the Walnut Street Theatre in Philadelphia, *Around the World in 80 Days* at the St. Louis Municipal Opera Theatre in Missouri, and

Shout Up a Morning at the La Jolla Playhouse in California and the world-famous John F. Kennedy Center in Washington, DC.

Angie's first big break came in 1982 when she cast as one of the street urchins in the original Off-Off-Broadway production of the *Little Shop of Horrors* musical at the WPA Workshop. The show was a smash hit and she continued with the show when it moved to the larger Off-Broadway Orpheum Theater. The musical was so successful, it went on to become a movie, years later.

In 1985, the most amazing thing happened. Angie was cast as the lead in a Hal Prince Broadway musical called *Grind* opposite Ben Vereen. She was amazing and received rave reviews. Muriel and I, of course, flew in for the opening. We were so proud of our daughter! She had worked so hard for so long, developing her skills and pursuing her dream, and it had all paid off.

That year, for her work in *Grind*, Angie was nominated for a Tony Award for Best Performance by a Featured Actress, a Drama Desk Award for Best Performance by a Featured Actress, and a Theatre World Award for Outstanding Broadway Debut. Angie invited one of her closest friends from high school, Willy Falk, to be her date for the big night of the Tony Awards. Willy and Angie had starred in many musicals and plays together at Punahou, and had both dreamed of one day hitting it big on Broadway. When they were in high school, they had made a promise to be one another's dates if they were ever nominated for a Tony Award, and true to her word, Willy was Angie's date on her big night.

Muriel and I threw a party in Hawaii the night of the Tony Awards. We bought a *Grind*-decorated cake from Leonard's Bakery and planned to celebrate with a big dinner, whether she won a Tony or not.

That afternoon, we received calls from New York that Angie had won both the Tony and Drama Desk Awards! Hawaiian time is five hours earlier than New York, so the program aired on local television five hours after it had actually happened "live" in New York. We began receiving calls every hour for five hours after she won as friends called when the ceremony was broadcast in their time zone.

We wanted everyone to see her winning the Tony at our party, so we didn't tell our guests we knew she had won. When the ceremony finally aired locally, and Ben Vereen opened the envelope and read Angie's name as the "Best Featured Actress in a Musical," we all screamed in delight and applauded as she walked up to the mic. Angie gave a great thank you speech, and we clapped along with the audience.

The next day, Wayne Harada, our local paper's theater critic who knew Angie from her many performances in Hawaii, wrote a column in the local newspaper about her eventful night, our cake from Leonard's Bakery, and our party. Word got around!

After Angie's Tony Award, she began getting cast in leading roles. Once, when Muriel and I were driving to see Angie starring in *Anything Goes* at State College in Pennsylvania, we saw a car full of students drive onto the highway on-ramp without stopping and making sure the way was clear. Tragically, an oncoming truck was unable to stop and crashed directly into their car, killing or injuring everyone inside. I was behind the truck, and I had been forced onto the shoulder of the road, fearful that the truck might roll over.

I ran up the hill to a restaurant to call 911, my heart in my throat, but the police were already on their way. I ran back down to the accident to help out if needed. The police had arrived and told me to keep back because of the possibility of the car exploding. I stayed to confirm to the officers that the truck driver had in fact put on his brakes but the kids drove into the truck because they were talking and did not stop at the stop sign.

We tried to enjoy Angie's performance that evening but were very upset by the accident. We shared with her what had happened on the highway to the theater. The incident was a reminder that we were no longer able to protect our precious children. They were on their own and we just had to trust that they would make good decisions to ensure their own safety.

In the 1980s, Angie also had the opportunity to work with Jerome Robbins on two shows, *West Side Story* and *Jerome Robbins Broadway*. Angie always said that having the opportunity to work with industry giants like Jerome Robbins was incredibly meaningful in her career.

In 1988, Angie was cast in an Off-Broadway production of a musical revue called *Blues in the Night*, which featured torch songs and blues music from the likes of Duke Ellington, Bessie Smith, and Johnny Mercer, among others. The other three performers were Carol Woods, Brenda Pressley, and Lawrence Hamilton. The musical was conceived

and directed by Sheldon Epps, and this particular production opened at
the Minetta Lane Theater in New York City. Muriel and I flew in from
Hawaii to catch the show. Angie was fabulous in this outstanding show!

Leilani would go on to perform in several productions of *Blues in the
Night* over the years. In one such production, the cast was invited to
perform in Japan, where there is deep appreciation for jazz. Seeing as
this was in the general neighborhood of Hawaii, I flew to Japan to spend
some quality time with Angie and see the show. I reached out to the
New Sanno US Military Hotel and arranged for the cast to have a
Sunday buffet lunch there. The performers in the show were delighted!
They were tired of Japanese food and longed for a classic American
buffet. The hotel manager was thrilled to have American "stars" from a
New York City musical at her buffet. She went all out, advertising the
show and the fact that the cast would be attending the buffet lunch the
following Sunday. I helped the cast travel by subway to the New Sanno
Hotel to give them the experience of mingling with the local people. On
the subway, some of the Japanese riders came over to get autographs
and mentioned seeing the play advertised on Japanese TV. I'm not sure
they had ever seen so many black people together at one time.

When we arrived at the hotel, we were met by a large crowd at the
buffet who gave the cast a standing ovation. We enjoyed the American
buffet very much. Even though we were in the middle of Japan, eating
American food, and surrounded by so many American diners, it felt as
though we were back in the US.

For some reason, the Japanese theater officials took a strong liking
to me. I got the impression they were surprised to see a father come so
far to be with his daughter and wanted to honor me. They invited Angie
and me to dinner one evening and presented me with a special clip-on
badge that would authorize me to enter the theater for free anytime I
liked. At the next day's matinee performance, I walked to the front
entrance, and the ticket girl bowed and ushered me in. I sat in the back
and later found a vacant seat down front after intermission.

The following day, I entered the theater from the stage door. A large
security guard was manning the entrance and when he saw me, he
bowed and ushered me in. I thought, *Wow! This badge is really something.* I
was treated like a VIP. After I returned to Hawaii, Muriel decided to fly

out to Japan to see Angie's show during her school break. I gave her the badge to wear, so she could experience being a VIP too.

Angie had always thought of the time she had spent cooling her heels in Hawaii doing local theater while in college as a missed opportunity. She gradually came to understand it was a tremendous gift. Productions in Hawaii were always cast multi-racially—out of necessity; the performing arts population was simply a reflection of the population on the island.

Angie was routinely cast in leading roles she would never have had the opportunity to play anywhere else in the country. In the 1980s, color-blind casting was rare, if not unheard of, on the mainland. It wasn't until Angie moved into mainstream theater in New York, and came face to face with restrictive, racialized casting, that she realized she had been afforded a priceless opportunity many of her black peers in theater had not. The training she received as a beneficiary of multi-racial casting in Hawaii allowed her to bring a breadth and depth of experience to every role she auditioned for in New York.

After Angie's great success in the theater scene in New York, she decided to make a move out to Los Angeles. There she met her future husband, Larry, did a nightclub act, and explored TV work. After she got married and had John and Lauren, she began to focus on more flexible work. Eventually she broke into a very specialized line of work: doing voiceovers or "descriptive audio tracks" for video games, television shows, and films. These tracks are used by those who are blind or partially blind. The speaker provides a verbal description of the action transpiring on the screen.

In the end, Angie made her way, on her own terms, and achieved extraordinary success. She believed in herself and pursued her dreams despite the skepticism of others and the obstacles along her way. Perhaps our greatest opportunity as parents is to simply allow our children the freedom to pursue their dreams—no matter how farfetched they seem. Who knows what potential lies in any one of us to achieve the unimaginable?

AL JR.

Al Jr. was an amazing athlete throughout high school. He excelled at soccer and was the star wide receiver on the football team. We loved going to his soccer and football games just as much as we enjoyed Angie's performances on the stage.

Al Jr. also loved to surf! He had grown up surfing, and it was one of his passions. Surfing was one of the most important things in his life for several years.

As a young black male, he faced more challenges than his sisters did growing up, and Damien High School, a private Roman Catholic all-boys college preparatory school, wasn't the easiest environment. The Irish brothers who ran the school tended to be pretty strict with the boys.

Al Jr. was less academically focused than Angie or Kim. When he graduated from Damien High School, we were very proud, but no clear path seemed to present itself for what was next. We knew that Al would have to further his education beyond high school and urged him to go to college.

The summer after Al graduated from high school, he took some time off. He hung out at home, surfed with friends on the North Shore, and took a part-time job as a painter in the Pacific Village neighborhood where we lived at the time. As summer passed, it became increasingly clear that the surfing lifestyle was unsustainable and that Al would need to get a real job and step into his future. His mother and I sat him down for a heart to heart talk. We told him that we were proud of him for being a good person, but that in order for him to be successful in life, he would need to learn a marketable trade, join the military or go to college. Little did we know that he would end up achieving all three of these things.

Al elected to strike out on his own and try to learn a marketable trade. Muriel's sister, Jeffrey, lived in Phoenix, Arizona where her husband, Archer, owned a carpet company. Archer agreed to let Al sign on as an apprentice laying carpet. Al had always been a hard worker, but nothing had prepared him to work for his Uncle Archer. Along with Archer's work crew, Al found himself working 12 hour days, 6 days a week, sometimes working past midnight to complete a job. After a year or two of laying carpet in the Arizona heat, Al, had enough of the trade vocation and decided to come home.

Al took a couple of different jobs when he returned to Hawaii, but soon decided it was time to kick-start his career. On January 20th 1981,

Al Jr. followed in my footsteps and joined the Air Force. He had scored high on the aptitude test and signed up for a career in electronics. Al completed his basic training in San Antonio, Texas and his specialty training on Lowry Air Force Base in Denver, Colorado, somewhat disappointed that within the field of electronics he was assigned a specialty loading bombs and munitions on fighter air craft.

Al's first duty station was in Germany at Spangdahlem Air Base. He decided to live off base in a small village called Duttledorf, where he played soccer with the locals, got to know the people in the village and became proficient speaking German. After serving in Germany, Al Jr. was stationed in Denver. He worked his way up through the ranks, receiving training and education along the way, and was able to cross train into Avionics, his true area of interest. Al learned to repair flight and navigations computer systems on F-111 aircraft and, ultimately, became an Avionics Instructor, training and supervising personnel in the inspection and maintenance of Air Force aircraft radar and weapons control systems.

KIM

Kim always loved animals! She grew up taking riding lessons and participating in a 4H program at Camp Smith's stables, a Marine base on the island. Her special charge was a rangy, dark bay thoroughbred named Taco. Kim spent many hours at the stable grooming Taco, cleaning tack, competing in horse shows, and taking lessons.

I took turns with other parents chaperoning the kids at the stable. I remember once we went on a twilight ride. We rode to a camping location where a campfire dinner of steak and beans was prepared and waiting for us. Then, we rode back to the stable before dark. I was glad to share the ride with my daughter and her friends.

One night, during her high school years, Kim went to a dance with a boy, but did not come home at the agreed upon time. We tracked down the home phone number of the boy she had left with, but he said he had dropped her off at our house. Now we were really worried.

We kept calling around to her friends to see if she had gone to one of their homes, until we finally got ahold of one girl who said Kim might be at the stable because her horse was ill. I raced up to the stables and found Kim taking care of her horse in the middle of the night. I just held her close, relieved she was okay.

"Kim, why didn't you call me? We have been worried for hours," I said.

"Sorry. I just wasn't thinking straight. As soon as I heard Taco was sick, I drove over here."

I said I would have taken her to the stable, and we could have brought our sleeping bags.

Muriel gave Kim a hard time when we got home for causing us so much worry. But nothing could come between Kim's love for that horse.

One year, Kim had the opportunity to ride in the King Kamehameha Day Parade as a pa'u rider. In this parade, each of the Hawaiian Islands is represented by a group of six or seven riders led by a woman representing a princess and her court. Kim rode as an attendant in the group, representing the island of Kahoolawe, the smallest of the eight islands.

The pa'u riders compete with one another and are judged as a team on their costumes and the floral adornments on their horses. The costumes are typically lavish and grand, often made of silk or velvet. That year, Kim's team decided to go for a more natural, authentic look. The fabrics for the women's gowns were cotton and homespun. The headdresses, leis, and garlands that hung around the horses' necks were made with gray Spanish moss, in keeping with the colors for the island of Kahoolawe. Kim's team won first place in the competition! Kim's riding instructor, a woman named Marty Strasburg, came to be a tremendous mentor to Kim, teaching her to ride but also introducing her to the world of showing cats. Marty owned a cattery of about twenty-five cats, and Kim would help her groom and care for them.

Kim had asked if she could have a pet at least a million times, but Muriel had always refused her request. When Kim's mentor, Marty, offered to give her one of her older show cats, Muriel realized she could no longer put Kim off. Hera was a double grand champion named after Zeus' wife. This cat was so smart. When Kim was not home, she put Hera in her room where Hera was supposed to stay. Sometimes Hera would wander into the living room. I would say, "Hera, you know you are supposed to stay in your room. Go back to your room." She would respond with a few meows before turning around and sauntering back into Kim's room. I think she was cursing me out, but I don't speak cat, so what do I know?

Once, Marty recruited Kim to stay at her house and take care of her cats and her dog, an imposing Doberman pinscher named Cass, for a week while she was on vacation in France. Kim was just sixteen at the time and driving. We decided to give our permission for Kim to undertake this enormous responsibility—grooming the cats, making sure they each got their homemade, specialized diet, and walking the dog. Kim later said this was one of the most formative experiences of her life; having someone trust her enough to leave her to care for their most precious possessions.

In 1979, Kim competed in a local beauty pageant, Miss Black Teenage Hawaii, which was sponsored by the Alpha Phi Alpha fraternity (the same one I was part of in my college days). The pageant was created to promote black pride in our youth. On the one hand, the fact that Hawaii was a diverse, mixed-race society where dark skin was not a liability was a unique and positive experience for our children. On the other hand, we wanted to make sure our children fully understood that they were African American and viewed that fact with pride.

For her talent in the pageant, Kim recited a passage from *The Autobiography of Miss Jane Pittman*, and for her activity, she wore the dress riding gear used by riders competing in horse shows. She won the competition and went on to compete in the national pageant in Norfolk, Virginia. She won fourth runner-up in Norfolk and received a beautiful set of luggage, just in time for her to go off to college.

From the very beginning, Kim was determined to attend college on the mainland. She knew it would be a financial challenge and so she carefully researched financial aid options, had us fill out the necessary applications, and applied to a number of schools. She was a strong student and was confident that she would qualify for aid at some of these schools.

Kim was accepted at all of the schools she applied to, including Stanford University in California, but Georgetown University in Washington, DC offered the best financial aid package, which consisted of a combination of scholarships, grants, and loans that Kim would have to pay back. She would also need to work all four years in the campus work/study program. She was overjoyed!

After graduating from Punahou High School, in the fall of 1980 Kim was off to Georgetown to study at the School of Foreign Service. Muriel and I saw Kim off with flower leis, hugs, and kisses. Our baby was all grown up.

It was bittersweet. We were suddenly empty nesters, now that our last child had departed. We continued to pray for all of our children's safety and well-being, as we had all their lives. Now our prayers had a new meaning. They were all away from our blessed home and out on their own in the world.

We have often reflected on all those years we struggled and sacrificed to give our kids the best education possible. We shared our beliefs and values through words and deeds. Now that they were gone, we hoped they would remember everything we had tried to teach them. We couldn't wait to share their future adventures in life. We were prepared to travel to the ends of the earth to visit and support them. We hoped they would remember us and keep us in their lives. All we could do was cry and pray—as I am doing now in reflection. God is always so good.

CITIZENS OF THE WORLD

Muriel and I suddenly found ourselves alone in Hawaii for the first time since we had arrived in 1957. Angie was in New York acting in theater, Al Jr. was in the Air Force, and Kim was in college in Washington, DC. For Muriel and me, it was a time of transition. I have never been able to remain static for long, and I began to plan our next adventure.

We knew that Kim was planning to study abroad in France during her junior year, and Al Jr. just happened to be stationed in Germany during the same period. This was a good time for a change, so I applied for a teaching job with the US Department of Defense to teach the children of US servicemen on a military base in England. This assignment would allow Muriel and me to be closer to at least two of our children.

I got the job, and so we embarked on a journey to RAF Wethersfield, in England. The US government shipped Muriel, me, our car, and furniture to England, and our exciting two-year adventure began.

When we first arrived on August 20, 1981, Frank, the principal of my new school, met our plane and welcomed us. Frank was a slender man about my height. He appeared to be happier to see Muriel than me because he happened to be looking for a substitute teacher at the school.

RAF Wethersfield is located about seventy miles northeast of London in an area known as East Anglia. The area around Wethersfield was quaint and picturesque, with rolling green countryside lined with hedgerows. It felt as though we had been transported back in time two hundred years.

We moved into a very small, three-bedroom home in The Village at Wethersfield called Hathor House. Our village was so small that homes had names instead of numbers. We had milk in bottles delivered to our door, and a man came by the house once a week to collect the bottles. The refrigerator was very small, the size we would have in our bar at home, so we had to go to the grocery store more often. We kept much of our furniture in storage until we could find a house large enough to accommodate it.

We bought a new, compact British Mini Morris that got fifty-four miles to a gallon of gas, unheard of in the US at that time, and had the steering wheel on the right-hand side. As in England, people in Germany drive on the left side of the road. Muriel and I decided to always drive together until we got used to the system. Muriel did the driving, and I gave directions to our destination and kept us on the correct side of the road.

When our American car finally arrived, we found that it was too big for the English country roads, so we parked it and relied chiefly on our new little car. We only used our big American car for Muriel to drive to the market and stores in Wethersfield. The British called our car a "Yank tank."

I was assigned to teaching social studies to the sixth-, seventh-, and eighth-grade classes, and Muriel, who by then had over a decade of full-time teaching experience, was slated to substitute for a teacher who was about to go on maternity leave. Muriel would be teaching reading, language arts, and math to the fourth- and fifth-grade classes. We settled into our new home just before our three children arrived for Christmas.

Angie flew in after closing out a successful run of the *Bloomer Girls* musical at the Goodspeed Opera House in Connecticut. Her flight was diverted to Manchester Airport because of snow and arrived twenty-four hours late. Kim was now studying abroad in Montpellier, France, during her junior year at Georgetown, and so she flew up to England for Christmas. Al Jr. flew over from Germany the same day we picked Kim up at Heathrow Airport in London. We had lunch at a quaint restaurant named The Dog, nestled in the charming village of Finchingfield. It was British in every possible way, from the fish and chips on the menu to the dog snoozing contentedly next to the fireplace. We had such fun as a family over that snowy Christmas holiday, visiting Buckingham Place,

Big Ben, and other tourist sites in London. Our family was reunited. To this day, regardless of where we all live, we always try to be together over the Christmas holiday.

Frank, our principal, enjoyed collecting antiques. Even his home in the village was an antique; it was four hundred years old. I wanted to get him a special Christmas gift, so I looked around the local shops and markets, hunting for interesting British antiques. I finally found the perfect gift: a tin-like can that Queen Victoria had filled with chocolates and sent to the soldiers in the Boer War in the year 1900. Her message, written by her hand, was "I wish you a Happy New Year." He was so surprised at our Christmas party to receive such a meaningful gift. I paid less than $10 for the tin, but I recently saw this exact same tin selling online for $230.

One drawback of life in Wethersfield was the lack of a Catholic community. I set out to resolve this. First, I got a list from the personnel office and called a meeting of all the Catholics on base, and I proposed we hire a British Catholic priest to come and say Mass in the chapel. Military chapels are designed to be used by all religious denominations and typically contain a small room designed to be used as a Catholic Tabernacle prayer room where communion can be kept for emergencies, such as for people who are dying or too sick to come to Mass.

I wrote to the Air Force chaplain's office to help us get things started. The chief of Catholic chaplains in Europe responded by designating me the Catholic Administrator for the base. I volunteered my services for free. He gave me the authority to hire whomever I needed and buy whatever I needed to support a Catholic faith community in RAF Wethersfield. He gave me a checkbook and a book of instructions on how to pay a British Catholic priest for each service he provided for our parish. In this way, I created a Catholic parish from scratch in my new home.

I visited Father Banks from Great Dunmow Parish and talked him into providing service to our new parish. Father Banks was a soft-spoken man with a warm smile that immediately put me at ease. He would be paid for his service and was clearly surprised at how much money he could earn for his parish from the wealthy Catholic Yanks. Father Banks got permission from his bishop and soon began servicing our Wethersfield community.

To sweeten the deal, I promised Father Banks that we would replace the broken stained glass window in his church within ninety days and organized a big barbecue fundraiser to which we invited not just the Catholics but the Protestant community and the whole base. All of this helped publicize the fact that a new Catholic parish had formed in Wethersfield.

The base commander liked the idea of the barbecue because it brought the American and British communities together for a good cause. He directed the commissary to provide, for free, all the food, tables, chairs, and personnel to make the BBQ successful. As the event picked up steam, it started to get too big for me to handle, and I was grateful for his support.

In the end, we got the window replaced in two months, a month earlier than promised. God works in mysterious ways.

Father Banks was a great priest. The only problem was the American Catholic Church by then had implemented more reforms than the British, which was a bit more traditional. For example, I was training men and women to become Eucharistic ministers and help give communion during Mass. Father Banks asked, "Are we allowed, Al?" I said, "Yes, Father." I called the US chief of Catholic Chaplains and asked him to speak to Father Banks and to verify that this was common practice in America. I could tell Father Banks wasn't ready for lay ministers to handle the Consecrated Bread, and so I only allowed the lay ministers to minister the Consecrated Cup. Father Banks felt better, I think, about that, but he only permitted Eucharistic ministry to be performed by lay people in our parish.

The base commander's wife, Dolly, a gorgeous, American, guitar-playing country singer, volunteered to be the music director for our Masses, which were suddenly full of young GIs, both Catholic and non-Catholic, eager to worship in the jubilant new parish. If I had been in their shoes, lonesome for home, I would have come to hear Dolly sing, too. She was a terrific asset to our young parish.

The US chief of Catholic Chaplains visited us as often as he could. I noticed his eyes would tear up each time he left us. I think he was moved to see our little Catholic community thriving. We had no American Catholic priest, but we were doing just fine. It shows what a group of individuals can do when united in a desire to practice their faith. I was proud of our parish. I knew it would continue on when my two years in England were up and I returned to America.

Once we succeeded in that venture, it was time for the next project. One day, Muriel and I went to the British Commonwealth Institute, a large building featuring displays of all the countries in the British Commonwealth, to see the "Yam Festival," in which British and Nigerian teachers put on a wonderful production about Nigerian culture.

This inspired me to create a course in our school that would teach Nigerian culture to our students one hour a week. Many of our students were the children of African American families, and I thought this content would be culturally enriching. I wanted our kids to learn how to tie-dye costumes in the Nigerian patterns, learn to play Nigerian drums, and to perform a play based on the Nigerian story of how their god sent his son to create the Nigerian people and be their first king.

The British and Nigerian teachers at the Commonwealth Institute welcomed my idea with enthusiasm, and we applied for and received funding from the US Department of Education. The centerpiece of the program would be the play. My goal was to perform the play at our school and also at the Commonwealth Institute in London at the end of the unit. I hoped to use the project to reduce behavioral problems among students, create a high-energy activity that would get many students involved, and raise the average grade per child by one level. In my experience, behavior problems and academic performance are generally a reflection of low overall engagement in learning.

Everyone was excited about our project: the British and American education departments; the Nigerian, British, and American teachers; the children's parents; and most importantly, the children. We had one teacher in charge of costumes, another in charge of music and prop creation, and I was in charge of the play production. The kids could sign up to participate in the area of their choice. The production would feature a large ensemble cast. As the weeks went on, the whole school became excited about the performance.

So many students auditioned for the play that we decided to cast two students for each part. The criteria for casting were how well the student could act out the part and memorize the lines. The rules for participation were maintaining "C" work or better and having no behavior problems. The behavior problems disappeared immediately.

The kids improved in all their classwork to ensure academic performance did not disqualify them from participating.

The starring role in the Nigerian creation story was the son who came to earth as the founder and first king of the Nigerian people. We had to narrow it down to two boys: a black boy and a white boy. I picked the black boy. The white boy complained that I picked the black boy because he was black. I told him I appreciated that he had shared his views with me. So, I had the two boys audition before a panel of teachers and kids who had already been selected. The vote was unanimous: the black boy had the best audition. The white boy became his understudy. If the black boy could not go on, he would take his place. I observed that the students and parents appreciated that we took the time to make sure the casting was as fair as possible.

Just before our trip to London, we performed the play before the entire school and parent community. The children received a standing ovation. They were so proud! The teachers, the parents, and the school staff were so proud of them too!

The next morning, off we went to London. When I arrived at the Commonwealth Institute, the official there said I was lucky to be visiting today because an American group would be performing a Nigerian play. I said, "That's us! Where do we go?" She escorted us to the practice area.

The play was a resounding success. Afterward, a Department of Education official told me she had been skeptical that we could pull off such a production with kids in junior high, but she was impressed by the performances, the costumes, and the music. I confessed, "To be honest, I had no idea the performance would be this good either!"

When we returned to school, the teacher presented me and the other two teachers helping with the production with Certificates of Merit from the US Department of Defense Office of Education for completing a project that impacted the morale and grades of the students of our school.

After about five months at Wethersfield, Muriel and I moved out of Hathor House. A British noble, known simply as "the Duke," had a large, vacant, ranch-style house he had built for his parents who were now deceased. The rent was high, but we paid it because it was the only home available in the area that met our needs. We later petitioned for an increase in our housing allowance to pay for the larger home, which was actually a normal size by American standards. We received the increase as part of an adjustment of every teacher's rental allowance to accommodate the high rental cost in the area.

The Duke and his wife were present at our new home when our furniture arrived from storage. They were surprised to see our huge refrigerator with the water and ice dispenser on the outside, commonplace in US households, but a novelty there. As Muriel gave them a tour of the house, filled with our other American-sized furniture, the Duke's wife tripped along beside her, periodically chirping, "Lovely, lovely."

Meanwhile, Muriel and I continued to enlarge our social circle within the broader community. We became very good friends with the school principal, Frank, and the other teachers at school, but as a retired Air Force major, Muriel and I were also invited to numerous military parties. In this way, we soon met a number of British and American officers in the area and their wives. We, of course, also got to know our neighbors and various locals in town and became good friends with the Duke and his wife.

Muriel and I have always enjoyed entertaining, and we mixed and matched these disparate groups with wild abandon. Because we had the largest home in the area, our house quickly became the go-to gathering place. Many of my colleagues at school had no idea of my rank as a field officer and were surprised to see the military brass who would show up at our events in full formal dress attire. Those who were single in the military community thoroughly enjoyed meeting the many unattached, young teachers from America who would also often attend. We had a ball, introducing these various communities to one another.

Living and working in England was a special time for our family. Muriel and I finally got to do some traveling in 1981, flying to Rome and taking a cruise to Egypt. Earlier in our marriage, we had traveled quite a bit, but for the ten years prior to moving to England, we had mainly stayed put in Hawaii. It was fun to re-experience that sense of exploration and immersion in different cultures. Our time abroad kept us close to our kids, and we saw them perhaps more than we would have had we stayed in Hawaii while they were living in New York, Germany, and France.

During a three-day school break in October, we visited Al Jr. in Germany. We also had the opportunity to spend time with Kim in London. She rented a dorm at the London School of Economics in London the summer prior to her year studying in France, and we saw her occasionally, either in London or Wethersfield. Interestingly, her experience at the American embassy ended up dissuading her from pursuing a career in foreign service, something she had been on track to do up until that point. She found the work routine and boring. It's hard for young people to understand that you start at the bottom and work your way up—everybody has to pay their dues.

The following year, Kim began her studies at the University of Montpellier in the south of France, but she soon learned it's not easy living in a foreign country and speaking a different language 24/7.

One day, Kim called and said, "Nobody loves me!" I suspected she was homesick. So, I flew to France to spend some time with her. We took the train to Bordeaux on the west coast and then continued down to the Spanish border town of San Sebastian. San Sebastian was a lovely tourist town, situated right on the beach. We enjoyed sampling its sidewalk cafes and catching up over leisurely strolls. We were both so happy to reconnect and spend time together!

When I signed up for a two-year teaching contract in England with the Department of Defense, I assumed that Muriel and I would spend the entirety of the assignment together in England. But in the summer after the first year, Muriel informed me that she would have to return to Hawaii in order to fulfill her obligation to the Hawaii Department of Education. Had she remained away for more than one year—the term of the leave of absence she had been granted—she would have lost her job and, more importantly, her retirement status.

Needless to say, I was shocked and dismayed. I had been looking forward to spending the second year traveling together around Europe during various school holidays. I was facing a year alone and I was not happy, but there was nothing to be done. Muriel packed up and the military moved her back to Hawaii, where she rented an apartment (we had rented our home—lucratively—for two years). She returned to her teaching position at Waipahu Intermediate School that fall. With Muriel gone, our home and my life felt unbearably empty.

To make matters worse, one day I got a message informing me that Muriel was in the hospital and had undergone an emergency operation. Shock, fear, and devastation overtook me. I took an emergency leave from my job in England and flew home to Hawaii. I was shaken to my core when I finally was permitted to see Muriel. She was very weak and could barely hold my hand. She was very, very happy to see me, but I couldn't talk. I could only cry. I was devastated that she had gone through this medical crisis all alone.

The doctor said that the operation had been successful and that Muriel would fully recover. Muriel was my life, the wind beneath my wings. We were among the luckiest people in the world because we loved and needed each other. If I had lost her, how could I have gone on with only half a heart? Life would have had less meaning.

When I returned to my job in England, I was only half there. I had to work out my second year in England per the terms of my contract with the US government. Luckily, everything at Wethersfield School was going smoothly because I could only think of getting back home to Muriel. Everyone understood and made allowances. I did the best I could, but my heart just wasn't in it. Living alone in England that second year was one of the toughest years of my life.

Muriel flew back to England to be with me the summer after I completed my second year at Wethersfield. She had fully recovered, as the doctors had promised, and wanted us to spend time together in Europe before returning home.

Meanwhile, Frank had been assigned to a larger school, and he asked me to come with him to start a Nigerian project there. I told him our adventure in Europe was over, and we went home before summer's end.

COMING HOME

Upon returning to Hawaii, I began a job teaching fourteen gifted and talented students at the Red Hill Intermediate School in the fall of 1982. I taught eight seventh- and eighth-grade students one period and six fifth- and sixth-grade students another period. I also did some substitute teaching while at Red Hill. I had never taught gifted and talented students before. I started out assigning them regular work for students their age, but they were so smart, they completed the regular work in half the time. I began to devise more challenging activities to stimulate their intellect.

I was assigned one eight-year-old gifted girl, Margaret, for one period a day. Her mother complained to the school that regular classes were not meeting her daughter's needs. I noticed, right off of the bat, that she was a very curious little girl.

Margaret said, "Mr. Jones, I want to experience what being blind, deaf, and dumb is like." I turned the light off, kept the door open, and told her to be completely silent and close her eyes. I told her that I was going to be quiet too, and when she was ready, she should ask me to turn the lights back on. After a few minutes, she asked me to turn the lights back on.

I asked, "How was it?"

She replied, "It must be horrible."

I said, "It is not horrible if you are born blind and that's all you know. You don't really know what it is not to see, and you live day-to-day learning what you can. If you have your sight and then lose it, that would be horrible because you would remember how wonderful it was to see."

Margaret proceeded to tell me about her family life, speaking at length about her cat. I suggested she might want to submit a piece about her beloved cat to the student essay and poem anthology the school published each year. She clapped her hands and said she would!

Margaret wrote many poems and stories, and I helped her as much as I could. She and I proofread everything together. Her mother came to meet me one day and asked me what Margaret's limits were. I said I didn't know, but that I had been surprised by her achievements so far. Margaret was the youngest student to have ever had her work published in the school's book of student writing.

I also worked as a substitute teacher for a special-needs class at Pearl City High School for six months. I had a blind student, seven deaf and hard-of-hearing students, and a girl who was physically fifteen years old but mentally only five. I ordered a Braille typewriter for the blind student, with earphones that would sound out words typed correctly. I gave him work to do, and he would type his answers on typing paper. I tried to brainstorm fun activities to do with a blind student. For example, I taught him how to say good morning in different languages.

Each morning, I greeted him with "Sawasdee, Charlie!" He would answer "Sawasdee, Mr. Jones" in Thai. The next day, I might say, "Buenos dias" in Spanish or "Bonjour" in French or "Buongiorno" in Italian or "Guten Morgen" in German or "Ohayou gozaimasu" in Japanese. If I saw Charlie walking on campus, I would call out a greeting so he would hear it, and he would yell it back to me. In time, the other students near us started to yell it back too! That was fun. I wrote the greetings on the board, and the deaf students in my class began signing the greetings to me. That was how I learned sign language.

I had learned that the key to teaching kids was to start by engaging them with content that they found interesting. For example, I learned that the kids were unfailingly fascinated by card tricks, and so I began to teach them card tricks and have them write down the instructions. The parents were delighted that their children were having fun at school while learning to read and write. Other teachers would walk by and see all the students enthusiastically working very hard on their assignments. Little did they know that sometimes the kids were reading and writing about card tricks! The students also made a list of things they would like to learn, like reading star constellations in the sky. Children learn best when the subject matter is customized to their areas of interest. Once students became engaged in learning, I was able to introduce more complex and challenging content. As a teacher, I saw my responsibility as inspiring children to learn *something*, anything. In my experience, once the flame is lit, a child's innate desire to acquire knowledge is activated and self-motivation kicks in.

The students in a Japanese class requested me as their substitute teacher when their teacher was out for a week. The teacher had a Japanese assistant, but the school required a trained teacher in every class. The assistant helped me a lot by assigning the day's classwork and correcting the assignments that the students turned in.

Teaching exposed me to a variety of subjects and often forced me to adapt to unfamiliar environments, which of course was something I had been doing all my career. When I subbed for the Japanese teacher for a week, my Japanese was so bad that it provoked laughter from the students. Nevertheless, we had a wonderful class. They got all their work done and left the class in high spirits.

When I substituted for the hula teacher, I was similarly out of my depth. They laughed at my poor dancing. When men do the hula, their movements are not as graceful as the ladies but jerkier and masculine-looking. My movements were so jerky the girls started laughing. I said, "Let me try something different." Whatever I tried, I would make it look funny to keep them laughing. When the class was over, I said, "Thank God! I'm tired!" And I would fake panting as if I really was exhausted. They would leave the room laughing themselves silly.

One year I faced the difficult challenge of teaching three emotionally challenged boys. These boys were a handful because they were always antagonizing and fighting each other. I had to place each boy in a separate space with a partition to the right and left. This configuration allowed the boys to see me but not each other. This was the only way to keep the boys focused on their own activities.

Painting and other artwork helped keep the boys occupied when seated at a large table, and they could shoot baskets in the gym as long as each boy had his own hoop. Each boy had his own assigned computer in the computer room. When the boys arrived, the computers were already set up for a game or another activity by the computer room teacher. I was pleased to have a highly skilled computer teacher to assist me with the boys.

I videotaped all of the boys' successful activities to show their parents once a month. Their parents were surprised their sons were learning computer skills. I recommended the families buy a family computer, if possible, to enhance their sons' communication skills.

One boy was truly a whiz on the computer, and I urged his parents to enroll him in special lessons. Later in life, perhaps he could get a job doing computer work at home and might not ever have to go to an office where social interaction would be a challenge. Another boy was very good at kicking field goals. I knew he could be successful with that skill and play sports in high school. The third boy's handicap required professional help.

I had to constantly occupy the boys and keep them in their seats and away from each other. Whenever the boys came into contact with one another, they invariably antagonized each other and fighting soon followed. Whichever boy was not fighting became extremely agitated when fights broke out around him. Keeping the peace required constant surveillance and heading off problems well before they could become crises. After one semester of teaching emotionally challenged youth, my doctor recommended I get another job. I had been successful working with the boys, but I had not realized how much stress it was creating for me.

Despite the stress, my time teaching at Red Hill provided a needed transition back to island life from living in England. I picked up some new skills teaching both disabled and gifted and talented students. Both groups required tremendous creativity and focus. It was not enough to simply cover the basics and apply the same teaching methods for everyone. Each child had unique needs and progress had to be measured on an individualized basis. These experiences developed my expertise as an educator, and I continued to apply these lessons throughout my career working with young people. I learned that a little humor in the classroom went a long way when connecting with and energizing students. The teachers always told me how much their students enjoyed my antics and shared how pleased they were that their lesson plans were completed in such a positive and inspiring way.

Soon after I left the military, I was informed that I had been selected to participate in the Agent Orange health study at Scripps Hospital at La Jolla, California. During the Vietnam War, the Army had sprayed Agent Orange, a chemical defoliant, from planes to kill the vegetation on the ground below and thus expose the enemy's hiding places. The so-called "Ranch Hands" (the servicemen who carried out these operations) started developing medical problems. Some of the crews from the Air Force who flew the Ranch Hands were having medical problems too. Therefore, the military was carefully monitoring the health of any personnel who might have been impacted.

Every two years, the study group was required to make a trip to the Scripps Hospital for testing. I wasn't showing any symptoms, but since I was on a crew that had transported the Ranch Hands, I was included. Participants were authorized to bring a companion on the trip to La Jolla, so Muriel came with me. We came to view the trip as a bit of a paid vacation every two years. But, needless to say, the whole thing was disconcerting, and I hoped my health wouldn't be affected. Only time would tell.

Even though the kids had long since moved away from home, Muriel and I tried to support them whenever we could. Family was always at the center of our lives.

Angie's career was on fire. We flew out to New York City to catch the opening of her nightclub act. She was marvelous! She sang a few of her Broadway songs and Hawaiian songs too. Many of her friends from Hawaii and New York were there, along with regular patrons of the club, and it was so much fun to catch up with them.

My favorite number was "E Ku'u Morning Dew," a song about waking up in the morning and smelling the flowers of Hawaii. Angie (or Leilani as she was now known) sang in Hawaiian and English, which evoked powerful memories of our home. We had gardenias and other flowers growing outside that filled the house with their fragrance. We lived at the foothills of the Ko'olau Mountains, and the wind blew so hard sometimes it would knock things over in the house. We kept the front door open often, to catch the fragrant winds. My daughter's soulful voice brought back the fragrance and feeling of this moment.

Meanwhile, after about fifteen years in the Air Force, Al Jr. experienced a major career transition. In 1994, as the military was going through a round of cutbacks, Al was offered the choice to separate from the military with incentive and partial retirement benefits. The skills he had gained in his years of military service were highly marketable and when Intel offered him a job working in one of their microprocessor manufacturing facilities, paying double his Air Force salary, he jumped at the opportunity. Al moved from Colorado to Oregon for the new job. He was very successful at Intel, a world class high tech company that offered him terrific pay and benefits, including allowing him to complete a dual Bachelor's degree in Business and E-business. Al achieved all three of the goals we discussed all those years ago when he was finding his way in Hawaii.

For years and years, we prayed that Al Jr. would meet someone special to share his life with. Finally, while in Portland, Al Jr. met a lovely young neonatal nurse through a religious website and fell in love. We were elated! Kathleen had a peaches-and-cream complexion, reddish-blonde hair, and warm, blue eyes. Kathleen and Al Jr. both had a very strong faith orientation and we knew that would ground their relationship. We saw how much Kathleen loved Al Jr., and we loved her at first sight! We were delighted that Al Jr. had finally settled down.

Kathleen's family was wonderful, too. They were as happy as we were that Kathleen and Al had found one another. We all met in Oregon for the wedding and Kathleen's family prepared a lovely wedding reception for the young couple. I was so happy to see Al Jr. married and thanked God for his blessings.

Kim graduated from Georgetown University in May 1984. Muriel and I flew in for the ceremony, excited to see our youngest daughter achieve this milestone and begin to make her way in the world. Kim moved up to New York and found a job on Wall Street working for Salomon Brothers. After a few years, she returned to school and earned an MBA from Columbia Business School. She was recruited by General Mills, headquartered in Minneapolis, Minnesota, and after five years in New York she moved to the Midwest to begin a career in brand management.

Our children's lives were taking them far from us, but they always managed to come home for Christmas or we all gathered together somewhere else. We did our best to stay in touch with the kids wherever they were living, talking by phone, visiting occasionally, celebrating their successes and commiserating with their challenges.

We also remained close to my DC family. My mother had eight sisters, and throughout our childhood had made a point of taking my brother and me around to visit her sisters and their families several times a year. As we grew into adulthood, my mother became absolutely committed to ensuring that her sister's families all knew one another and stayed in touch. She was the oldest living sister; she had her health and tremendous energy. She was the fire behind planning regular family reunions. My mother would meet with representatives of each of her sister's families to work out the details of these family events.

One such family reunion was held on a weekend in July 1987, at a hotel ballroom in Bushwood, Maryland. My mother's sisters had large families and over two hundred people attended from the Curtis, Dyson, Jones, Outlaw, Taylor, and White clans. My mother was the matriarch of our extended family by this time and always the life of the party. She was short and fiery and was known to dance on top of tables. Her childhood nickname had always been "Stump," on account of her diminutive stature. On special family occasions, such as this, my mother was always dressed well, typically wearing a dress, stockings, a hat, church shoes, and a large pocketbook.

At the start of the reunion, my mother shared her reflections on the importance of family and her joy at having all of us gathered together. My younger brother Robert led us in the song "Trees." He would sing a line, and the rest of us would sing it back to him. Robert was a little buzzed from drinking, so I knew he was in trouble when he got to the line, "Songs are made by fools like me, but only God can make a tree." And we sang, "Songs are made by fools *like him*!" And we all pointed at him. I said, "Let's bring it on home!" And we all stood up and sang, "But only God can make a tree!"

Then we all clapped and went up to congratulate Robert on the great song he'd selected. Robert was laughing so hard his sides were hurting. "I walked into that one, didn't I?" he hooted.

These reunions were joyous occasions in which we played cards, got to know distant relations, laughed, ate good food, and reminisced about days gone by. We always had a priest attend and provide a Mass at the end of the reunion on Sunday to pray for those who had passed or were ill and unable to attend. It was good to reconnect with kinfolk and be reminded that while we didn't see each other often, we were still family.

A couple of years later, my brother Aloysius and I hosted an extended family reunion in Hawaii. A full busload of assorted family members was able to make the trip. My daughter Angie and I arranged most of the activities. We rented a bus and made a list of the special places on Oahu that we wanted to share with our guests. We included many of the typical tourist stops but also some lesser-known gems such as Queen Emma's Royal Summer Palace and the Matsumoto Shave Ice store in Haleiwa.

We hosted a big party at our home, setting up tables and chairs outside to accommodate the sixty guests that attended. Our friends and neighbors brought exotic dishes, and some of them played music and danced Polynesian and Asian cultural dances. Anyone who wanted to join in and try their moves was invited to do so. Years later, our mainland family was still talking about their wonderful trip to Hawaii.

In 2000, I received a heartbreaking phone call. My younger brother Robert had suddenly died. He was only sixty years old. I flew from Hawaii to Washington, D.C. immediately to help in any way I could. I had not realized my brother had been ill for some time, so his passing was a huge shock. Even those in our family who were aware that Robert had been ill had not realized he was *that* ill. Robert didn't like going to doctors.

Robert was tall and slender and always dressed well. He had an infectious laugh and a flamboyant, lively personality. I could not believe he was gone. Robert had been living in our family home and taking care of Mother for many years, something he had always intended to do; he had never married.

Robert worked as a professional chef for decades. He was the chef at a restaurant in DC called Mr. Henry's for many years. Robert shared my passion for travel and took short-term jobs cooking on cruise ships going to Europe and South America. He later became a travel agent for a large travel company and would sometimes take my sister Beulah with him when he traveled for free, checking out hotels, cruises, and restaurants. Once, the two of them traveled to Paris for a weekend. They had great times traveling the world together.

Beulah, who lived in DC, took charge of making the funeral arrangements. I stayed at the house with Mother and the two of us shared some precious time together.

Mother and I went to Safeway one day to buy groceries. Mother enjoyed walking around looking at all of the items on display. We decided to buy green beans, and Mother started breaking off the ends before putting them in her bag.

I exclaimed, "Mother, you can't do that. You can break those off when we get home."

The clerk just chuckled and said, "It's okay—at her age, she can do whatever she wants."

We paid for our items and returned home. We decided to have fried chicken, cooked green beans, mashed potatoes, and gravy for dinner.

"I'm going to make biscuits," I told my mother.

"That's going to take too long," she said. She was accustomed to making biscuits from scratch, which was a bit of an undertaking.

Well, when we sat down to eat, there on the table was a plate of delicious, warm biscuits. My mother gaped in amazement, took a bite out of one of the biscuits, and asked, dumbfounded, "How did you do that?"

"Pillsbury makes biscuits you can bake in fifteen minutes," I explained, laughing. She could not get over how good those biscuits were.

At the funeral and burial, I was overwhelmed by memories of Robert throughout the years—playing cards, preparing meals for the family, being silly, and just having fun. Most of all, I remembered Robert as a little boy sitting on my lap. He was a kind and gentle soul, beloved by the mother, brothers, sisters, nieces, and nephews he left behind.

I cleaned my brother's room thoroughly and helped my mother pack up his things. As Mother and I went through his closet, she picked up his long fur coat and said, "I want this." The coat didn't fit her, but I just said, "You go, girl!" and put the fur coat in her closet. My sisters and their children came to the house to take whatever they wanted of Robert's things. I called the Salvation Army to pick up what was left. My brother was gone.

YOUTH MINISTRY

One of my true passions was volunteering for the Catholic Church in Hawaii. In my home church, Our Lady of Good Counsel, I taught adults who wanted to join the church and adults who were Catholic who wanted to receive the sacrament of Confirmation, through the church's Rite of Christian Initiation of Adults (RCIA) program.

One day, in 1995, I visited Sister Kathleen, the Diocesan director of Religious Education to see if there was more I could do to serve. Sister Kathleen was an absolute dynamo within the faith community on the Hawaiian Islands. She told me that I was the answer to her prayers. The director of Youth Ministry for the Catholic Archdiocese of the Hawaiian Islands had just passed away, and she had been praying for someone to come and take his place. She asked if I would be willing to take on this position.

Cautious about overcommitting myself and feeling underqualified, I told her I would be willing to serve as the "interim" director of Youth Ministry until she could find someone else to fill the position. Sister Kathleen just smiled and nodded. I declined to draw a salary for this position. I said I would work Mondays through Fridays from 8 a.m. to noon—or longer if a problem required more time to solve. I later learned that once she had convinced me to take the job, Sister Kathleen stopped looking for a permanent replacement.

As part of my role leading youth ministry, I helped oversee the Hawaiian folk Mass, which took place on the beach on Saturday evenings. A big part of that event was the Offertory Procession, where an elaborate procession of teens brought gifts representing the various islands. They also wore the colors of their respective island and carried a "kāhili," a long pole with a feather display at the top that was in that island's color. The feather pole was a symbol that was carried to identify a member of the Hawaiian royal family in the past. Their display garnered a lot of collections, especially from the tourists.

Those attending the Mass sat on mats on the sandy beach. The liturgy of the Mass was printed in a colorful booklet in both English and Hawaiian. The booklet was passed out to everyone free of charge as a souvenir.

I always stayed around after Mass to greet everyone and answer their questions. I explained that when the Catholic priests first came to Hawaii, they gave the Hawaiian elders a statue of Jesus, Mary, or one of the saints to natives who converted to Catholicism, understanding the importance of religious icons in their prior faith tradition. The statue reminded them of that person who they could pray to. The priests incorporated traditional hula dance into Mass and they celebrated the Mass in English and Hawaiian. These concessions help smooth the transition from native religions to the Catholic faith. The folk Mass was a way to remember the beginning of the Catholic faith in Hawaii and share it with the tourists.

I loved being the director of Youth Ministry, which united my three passions (teaching, kids, and my Catholic faith) in one job. The job entailed ensuring that the churches in the diocese had active youth ministries with adult leaders equipped to steward youth faith formation. I saw this role as a sacred responsibility and decided that to do it well, I would need to bring the very best practices in Catholic youth ministry to our kids in Hawaii.

I attended the three-day annual Los Angeles Religious Education Congress in Anaheim, California, where I participated in three workshops a day to learn best practices in youth faith engagement. I disseminated these practices widely back in Hawaii and later expanded my practice to Samoa and greater Polynesia to strengthen youth ministry in those locations.

I was deeply committed to keeping the Catholic faith alive in ways that would excite and energize the kids. I remember having the teens participate in Mayor Frank Fasi's annual Thanksgiving Day Lunch for the Poor at the Convention Center. The Salvation Army organized everything. The city employees, high school teens, Catholic teens, teen clubs, and others provided the manpower. The city buses picked the poor up from the streets of Honolulu and transported them to and from the convention center. High school bands and hula dancer clubs provided the entertainment. My brother's daughters, Jackie and Jeanette, were among those dancing the hula. The turkeys and the other dinner items were cooked in restaurants and school cafeterias and taken to the center. Some teen groups volunteered to handle clean-up. It was a magnificent display of charity, community, and goodwill, and the participation and coordination of all these different groups made the execution successful.

Our group from Our Lady of Good Counsel signed up to serve the tables. Our vision was to emulate Jesus Christ by feeding the poor. Between cleaning, serving, and other tasks, everyone had a role. My job, as supervisor, was to make sure our guests were fed as soon as they sat down and the area was cleared, cleaned, and made ready for the next group's arrival, after each group was done eating. Everyone worked calmly and efficiently and performed their tasks with joy. We were so proud to be a part of it all. We never forgot the importance of charity toward the poor, and volunteering at the luncheon became an annual tradition. The event was a powerful way to show the kids what our faith calls us to do.

My teens also participated in the Walk for Mankind, an annual eighteen-mile charity walk to raise money for the city's poor, for many years. We would start walking early in the morning and finish just before sundown. When we crossed the finish line, people would clap and cheer us on. We were tired and sore but happy to have finished.

On these walks, I invariably ran into students I had taught over the years. I remember once I ran into a blind former student named Donnie Pagador. She was passing out water bottles.

"Hi, Donnie!" I called out.

She exclaimed, "Mr. Jones? Oh, Mr. Jones. I'm so happy to see you!"

Crying, she ran around the table and into my arms and gave me a big hug and wouldn't let go. I ran toward her because I didn't want her to run into anyone or anything because she was totally blind. I started to cry too as I had not seen her for a while.

I was close with many of my students, but Donnie and I had a special connection. I met her while substituting in a music class at her school. My daughter Angie was assisting me that day by teaching the teens how to properly warm up their voices and by singing with them. Despite being blind, Donnie was very active and involved in everything. She was such an inspiration because she did not allow her disability to slow her down at all. My wife said that Donnie was the smartest student she had ever taught and received all As in her classes! She said that the students loved her and took turns guiding her to her classes and around the school. I loved Donnie like my own child.

Another faith walk I enjoyed was the Walk for Life, sponsored by our bishop, Bishop Ferrario (who later awarded me the "Our Lady of Peace Award" in recognition of service in catechetical ministry). In addition to parish youth and adults, I would often take my own children with me on these walks. The Walk for Life was intended to emphasize the value of the life of a newborn baby. The bishop was joined by the leaders of many religious and civic groups. Our Knights of Columbus posted themselves near him so that we could provide additional protection along with the policemen assigned. There were counter-protesters also present. After the speeches, we walked around the state capital area where people passed out water bottles.

I took thirty teens to World Youth Days in Denver in 1993. Pope John Paul II was going to attend. The newspapers wrote that the Pope would have a difficult time relating to American teens. The 860,000 kids and their chaperons who attended begged to differ. The young people loved the Pope! We met his airplane and cheered his arrival. The food was kid-friendly and included cold drinks from McDonald's. Though there was plenty of free water, the kids were fainting by the dozens because they were dehydrated; it was hot and we were at a high altitude. I ran around giving everyone bottles of water, which I insisted they drink immediately. One of the girls in my group fainted and had to be taken to the hospital. One of her friends went with her. They kept her overnight, but she was able to join us the next day.

There were many vendors selling pizza, hot dogs, hamburgers, and French fries for fifty cents each. I encouraged the kids to give any food they did not eat to the poor along the way.

In the evening, the Pope arrived by helicopter, stayed with the young people for a while, leading us in prayer, and then said good night and took off in his helicopter. We all slept in our sleeping bags with one plastic sheet under us and one over us in case of rain.

The next morning, the Pope arrived for Mass and speeches. He inspired the teens and young adults to be missionaries in their parishes and to volunteer for parish ministries focused on helping the poor and needy. When he left in his helicopter, World Youth Day was over. The kids were deeply impacted by the Pope's speech and walked back to our hotel singing songs along the way. When we returned home, we attended all the Mases on Sunday, thanking everyone for their support. The trip was a catalyst that drove enthusiastic youth participation in our parish ministries. We dramatically increased the numbers of teens and young adults engaged as parish lectors, special ministers for Holy Communion, choir members, youth club members, fiesta workers, and participants in other activities of the parish and community. The experience was so positive, I took another group to World Youth Day in Paris in 1997.

I was surprised to receive an invitation to the Hawaiian Islands Ministries workshops in 1997. There were leaders and teachers from all of the various Christian Ministries including our Catholic Church. I was invited to attend and receive the Nicodemus award for "Excellence, Creativity and Innovation in Christian Education." There were over five hundred people in the auditorium for this presentation. Sister Catherine was the Catholic member who had submitted my name to be recognized for my accomplishments in youth ministry. Receiving Nicodemus was a tremendous honor.

After receiving the award, I didn't have a moment to myself. Muriel and I would be having lunch, and someone would sit down to ask me questions about how to teach teens more effectively. I suddenly felt like a celebrity due to my expertise in teen faith formation. I was glad when the workshop was over and I did agree to several follow-up meetings to assist with other teen ministries. I was quite busy for a while. All those workshops I had attended at the yearly LA Religious Education Congress in California clearly paid off!

I had the opportunity to attend one last World Youth Day in Rome in August 2000. Two million teens were attending the event, many of them housed in dioceses on the outskirts of Rome, but since I had reserved our hotel early, we were in Rome proper.

The field at the vigil site had large screens broadcasting all of the activities, and each person could hear everything on their radio. Each person received a box of canned foods to eat at the vigil site, but you could buy affordable fast food too. The teens kept some of the food in their boxes and gave the rest to the poor families we passed on our hike to the site.

It took us hours to get to the site and find our spot. We spread a plastic sheet on the ground and set up our sleeping bags. We had another plastic sheet ready to shelter under in case of rain. We all had a booklet of songs and prayers in English we planned to recite that evening and through the night and early morning.

As before, the Pope arrived by helicopter at the altar site. We could see him from a distance because that area was on high ground. We could also see him clearly on the huge screens and hear everything in English on our radio. After the Pope gave the service, he said good night and told us he would see us at sunrise the next morning. He was then taken away by helicopter. I was tired and went to sleep. Some of the teens were sleeping, some were talking quietly, and others were softly singing.

One of the activities the kids enjoyed most was trading souvenirs with other kids attending the event from all over the world. We had brought small circular disks of cardboard with pictures of the Hawaiian royal kings and queens, hula dancers, and scenes of Hawaii to trade. They were similar to the bottle caps that used to be on bottles of milk. I was able to get hundreds of them free before leaving Hawaii when I shared that we would be giving them away to teens from around the world on World Youth Day. Our disks were in great demand.

After the event concluded, we returned to our hotel and finished the trip with a few other activities and tours we had planned in advance. We were all so glad to have traveled to Italy to spend time with the Pope and teens from all around the world. We again thanked everyone for their support and shared the highlights of our adventure in Rome with the Pope at all the Masses the following Sunday.

ADVENTURING

After years of flying for the Air Force followed by years of traveling internationally in retirement, you might imagine I had gotten my fill of travel, but you would be wrong. I still had places I wanted to visit or revisit, and other adventures that I wanted to explore. Although I was no longer on active duty, I could still fly for free on military aircraft when there were empty seats on a plane. The military called this type of flying "Space A," which stands for space available. Muriel tended to prefer to stay at home, so I often went adventuring on my own.

One of my favorite places to visit was Israel—a lifelong dream since I was a boy. In 1981, my wife and I visited the Dead Sea, and I floated in the water, which is famous for its high salinity and buoyancy.

That evening, we were looking out the window as the sun was about to go down. Suddenly, the street was empty of cars! Muriel said, *"Wow! What happened?"*

I said that it was Friday evening, and at sundown, the Jewish Sabbath starts. The Jews may not drive at all that night or all day Saturday. If anyone drove in the Jewish area, they would throw rocks at their car. All Jewish businesses were closed. If we wanted to eat or go shopping, we had to go to an Arab or Christian area in another part of the city.

We also stayed overnight at an Israeli kibbutz near the northern border. The kibbutz is governed by the members who meet and decide issues in a direct participatory democracy. This kibbutz decided to raise funds by inviting tourists to visit and stay in apartments overnight or longer. We toured the kibbutz and had our meals with the community. We watched and sometimes participated in the dances they performed. My wife and I, and other tourists, enjoyed the rare experience of being a part of a large Jewish community.

Although I often embarked on trips alone, I usually acquired traveling buddies along the way. On another solo trip to Israel, I was praying in the Garden of Gethsemane and felt my wallet moving. I turned around and spotted an Arab teenager trying to steal it, and I said, "Ibn al qayyim," which means "May Allah have mercy on him," and turned back around and continued praying.

When I had finished praying, the thief and his friends were standing nearby. I said "Allah Akbar," which means "God is great" in Arabic. They said, "Allah yehfazak," which means, "God bless you!" Suddenly, I became very emotional. I realized the young men were guarding the space to prevent anyone else from disturbing me. In an instant, they had changed from predators to honored protectors. God is great!

Once, I arrived in Israel and asked the cab driver to take me to the YMCA. After I got settled in, I thought I would walk around and maybe stop for a drink somewhere, but everything was shut down tight! Suddenly, I realized that I had inadvertently booked myself into the Arab YMCA located in an Arab neighborhood where there were no bars because Muslims do not drink in public places. I returned to my room and immediately booked a spot in the Israeli YMCA for the following night. The desk clerk said maybe the cab driver, seeing I was American, simply took me to the YMCA that was closest to the American Embassy. We both had a laugh about that.

On another trip, I was traveling Space A from Germany to Israel. On the flight, I had my maps out and was planning where I would stay and what sights I would visit. Suddenly a slim, white college student came over, sat next to me, and struck up a conversation.

He introduced himself, saying, "Hi, my name is Steve. I'm a student traveling alone, and I wonder if you might be willing to share a room with me because I can't afford one by myself."

I said, "Sure, but I do have a fixed itinerary. There are certain sites that I am planning to visit because I am preparing materials for my religious education class. I am planning to visit places where Jesus walked that I have not been to before."

He excitedly asked, "Do you mind if I tag along with you?"

Suddenly, the gentleman on the other side of me—an approximately fifty-year-old white man with an athletic build—jumped in and introduced himself. "Hi, I'm John, and I couldn't help overhearing your conversation. I'm traveling alone too, and if the three of us share a room together, we could probably get a large suite at a reasonable cost."

I declared, "That's fine by me," and the student readily agreed too. I was delighted because now my hotel expense would be one-third of what I had planned and looked forward to getting to know my new traveling companions.

We had a ball touring the places where Jesus had walked over two thousand years ago. I became the de facto tour guide and explained the importance of each site. I was able to record on video the sites that I would be sharing with my classes when I returned home.

My final destination was the Jordan River, and when we arrived at the site, John decided to take off his shoes and socks and wade in the water. He slipped and cut his leg badly. I took off my t-shirt and wrapped the makeshift tourniquet around the wound.

When we returned to our hotel, John called for medical aid. I was astonished to see an ambulance arrive within five minutes. They whisked John away to take care of his leg and brought him back later that day. I asked him, "Who are you? You have to be someone important to get such quick medical aid." John said his identification was classified. He was on vacation and just wanted to relax and enjoy himself. I wondered if he was a member of our intelligence community.

Later that evening, sadly, there was an explosion at one of the markets in town. Our trio went to check it out the next morning. When we arrived at the marketplace, Israel's first lady was visiting the explosion site and speaking with various people in the area. She was a beautiful woman—poised, articulate, and friendly—and surrounded by her security detail, reporters, and photographers. By chance, she came over and spoke to us, and we were immediately engulfed in her entourage. She noticed that John was injured and asked, "How is your leg?" John said, "Oh, it's fine. It's not serious." We chitchatted for a few minutes, and she left with her entourage.

I called Muriel and asked, "Guess where I am?" She named a few countries, and I said no. I told her I was in Israel. She said, "Get out of there. They bombed a marketplace there yesterday!"

"I know," I exclaimed, "we were just there today!"

The next day, the English newspaper described John as a heroic survivor, which needless to say, made him extremely uncomfortable. Evidently, the first lady had assumed that John had been injured in the explosion the day before. There was nothing we could do about it!

In the spring of 1992, I embarked on a cross-continental European rail journey with the goal of visiting two locations where Jesus' mother, Mary, had appeared to various individuals. I began my journey by hopping a military plane from Hawaii to Ramstein Air Force Base in Germany and boarding the train from there. My ticket was first-class, but I ended up traveling in second class most of the time because there were more people to talk to and play cards with. Many of the travelers were in their thirties and enjoyed conversing with older travelers who could answer their questions and provide useful advice or information.

My first stop was in Amsterdam. I checked my luggage at a storage facility and toured around until evening, at which time I boarded a train with the final destination to Paris, France, stopping off at Brussels, Luxembourg, and Strasbourg along the way. In each location, I toured for one day and then boarded a train heading toward Paris. I enjoyed meeting other tourists, having meals together, playing cards, and sharing our joy of traveling. I had learned how to sleep almost anywhere in the Air Force. I slept some nights on the train in a recliner seat and some nights in a hotel near the train station.

When I finally arrived in Paris, I rented a room near the train station and spent two days exploring many of the sites I had read about all my life but had not yet visited. From Paris, I went on to visit the cities of Tours and Bordeaux. When I was finally ready to leave France, I boarded a train for a long ride to Lisbon, Portugal. I was invited to join a group of card players. I knew how to play bridge and they needed a fourth person. I realized I had to tone down my bidding to match their ability. My partner and I were winning too much, so I tried to play to lose but couldn't. They decided to switch partners and that evened the game out.

I finally arrived in Lisbon, Portugal, where I visited the Our Lady of Fatima Catholic Church, the site where a miracle had transpired in 1917. Jesus' mother, Mary, had appeared to three children at this site after World War I and prophesied the coming of World War II. Mary told the children to ask everyone to pray for peace. There was a church at the site, which was filled with pilgrims from all over the world speaking different languages. On the day that I arrived, there were thousands of people in the area waiting to access the grotto where the Virgin Mary had appeared. Many were suffering from various afflictions and being transported to the site. I decided to walk along with a group of individuals in wheelchairs to see what would happen. As we were walking, I wondered, *Will any of these people be healed?* Some appeared to be praying intently. Others showed no outward indication that they believed they would be helped in any way. I noticed that some people left the site healed while others did not. I believed that those who prayed, had faith, and were in a state of grace, were healed. I was elated to stand on this sacred ground, as it fulfilled one of my lifelong dreams. Visiting the grotto was the highlight of my time in Portugal.

From Portugal, I traveled east to Madrid, Spain. When I arrived in Madrid, I checked into a hotel for three days. I went to the Palace of the Bulls to experience the most famous bullfighting arena in the world. During the bullfight, the matador entices the bull to attack his red cape, which is held very close to his body. When he has worn the bull out with charging his cape, he kills the bull with a special sword. I liked the drama of the bullfight, but did not like the killing. On another trip, Muriel and I visited Madrid and went to a bullfight. The matador was injured and we left. It was all simply too violent for us.

After Madrid, I caught a train to Lourdes, France, to visit the site where in the 1870s, Bernadette Soubirous saw Jesus' mother Mary. When she appeared to Bernadette, Mary asked her to tell everyone to pray for sinners and told her where to dig for water that would heal the sick who drank in faith. There was a huge cathedral at the site and on both sides of the building, there were many spigots where the sacred water from the site could be collected by the pilgrims. Once again, I witnessed many individuals who drank the water at the site be cured of their afflictions. A man who arrived on crutches after drinking the water was immediately healed and held his crutches above his head, rejoicing that he did not need them anymore. I saw this with my own eyes.

The saddest part of the visit was observing those who drank the water and were not healed. They were devastated. Many of them wept openly and I, too, began to cry, for their disappointment. It was such a painful thing to see. Visiting Lourdes was a powerful and moving experience that I have never forgotten.

After leaving Lourdes, I travelled to Geneva and Bern, Switzerland, before moving on to the picturesque, college town of Heidelberg, Germany. My tour included visiting a winery, where the wine was excellent. By the end of the evening, everyone was singing merrily. I joined in singing the songs that I knew. I found that wherever I went, I was warmly welcomed and, inevitably invited to join a group. I always felt accepted, maybe because American tourists brought American dollars with them wherever they went.

I boarded the train to Frankfurt am Main, Germany, my last stop. There was a military base there, and I checked in at the officers' quarters until it was time for my flight back to America. I was tired and ready to go home.

MILESTONES

We visited Kim in Minneapolis shortly after she moved there from New York to start working at General Mills and were delighted to see, with our own eyes, that she was happy and enjoying her new job.

A few years later, Kim called me to say that she met a wonderful young man, Stafford Nelson, whom she said was "like me," and that they loved each other very much. Angie had given Muriel and me the heads-up that Kim was dating someone and that he was white. I wondered, *How was he like me?*

I would find out for myself soon enough, as Kim decided to bring Stafford home for a visit the following Christmas. It was the first time she had ever brought a boyfriend home to meet us, so we knew he was important to her. Kim asked me to talk to Mom because she did not know how her mother would feel about her marrying a white man. Kim said that she knew I would like anyone she loved, but her mom was a wildcard.

Stafford pulled out all the stops to make a favorable first impression, including sending flowers to Muriel in advance. When Stafford and Kim arrived in Hawaii, Stafford was extremely courteous, attentive, and 100 percent committed to charming Muriel. Most importantly, it was obvious that he was very much in love with our daughter.

During that first trip, we had the opportunity to spend quality time getting to know Stafford. Kim, Staff, and I hiked to Diamond Head, and we took Staff sightseeing to Waimea Falls Park. We all fell in love with

Staff and were glad Kim had found someone funny, kind, and agreeable to be with. I guess he *was* like me! Praise the Lord!

Kim and Stafford were engaged the following year and returned to Hawaii that Christmas. Muriel and I decided to plan a huge engagement party, inviting all of our friends, Kim's friends, our Kailua family, and our neighbors to celebrate the joyous occasion.

Coincidentally, around the same time, Angie had met someone too! Larry Wilmore was an up-and-coming comedian when Angie met him shortly after moving to Los Angeles in 1989. Angie decided to bring Larry home to Hawaii for Christmas too, so both girls were home with their beaux.

Larry was terrific and clearly cared deeply for Angie. We all anticipated that a proposal was imminent—after all, it was Christmas—so much so that when Muriel made a massive, congratulatory banner for Kim and Staff's engagement party, it read: "Congratulations, Kim and Staff and Angie and Larry."

The expected proposal had not arrived by the date of the party, thus the banner had to be "corrected" on the fly. The alteration was barely adequate, but somehow we managed to conceal the embarrassing bits when the banner was unfurled and displayed prominently in the house. We had so much fun getting to know our future sons-in-law and sharing our beautiful island with them.

In 1992, we traveled to Minnesota to meet Stafford's parents, Valerie and Leroy Nelson. I don't think anyone really knew what to expect; we were so different from one another—or so we thought.

Valerie was Canadian and had grown up in white-glove society in Winnipeg, but had a bubbly personality and an irrepressible zest for life. She was a bit of a rebel for her era and had been a chemist and ballerina at various points in her life. She had met Leroy when they both worked for the old Northwest Airlines, he as a purser and she as a stewardess.

Leroy had grown up on a farm in rural Minnesota, like Muriel, but his parents had died when he was very young, and he had been raised by his sister. He struck out on his own when he was fifteen and made a life for himself.

We all hit it off immediately! As we got to know them, we realized we had a lot in common. We loved to play cards (Valerie was a bridge grand master, and Muriel and I had played bridge for years). As couples, we both loved to dance, and approached life with an open mind and a spirit of adventure. After meeting Stafford's parents, it was not hard to see why Stafford was such a wonderful person,.

Kim and Stafford were to be married on July 3, 1993, in Edina Morningside Community Church, so our extended family gathered in Minnesota for the occasion. Kim and Stafford's groom's dinner was particularly memorable. After we all sat down, but before the food arrived, Stafford's brothers and father each stood to toast the happy couple. After the last of the toasts, suddenly Angie's boyfriend, Larry, began to rise to his feet. *Not necessary and not appropriate,* I thought. Why would the bride's sister's boyfriend feel the need to say anything at this occasion? He was lucky to have been invited.

Painfully aware that Larry was a comedian by trade and fearful that he might try to say or do something "funny" (not the place!), Angie yanked downward on the tails of his coat as she urged, "Honey, sit down!"

Undeterred, Larry launched into a heartfelt talk about how special our family was and how much he had enjoyed getting to know the Nelsons. Nice to know, but speaking at all was a bit odd given Larry's weak tie to the whole affair.

Suddenly, Larry wrapped up his comments by expressing his desire to become *a part* of our extended family, producing a diamond ring and placing it on Angie's plate. We were all stunned into a shocked silence, and then the table erupted in shouts, screams, and laughter. Talk about drama! What an exciting surprise. We had kind of all been waiting for Larry's proposal, but he picked the moment it was least expected!

Angie and Larry got married one year later on May 28, 1994, at St. Charles Borromeo Catholic Church in North Hollywood, California. As a member of the prestigious St. Charles Borromeo Choir, Angie was able to get the entire choir to sing at her wedding. Both of my daughters wanted me to wear my full military dress uniform with medals at their weddings, and I managed to squeeze into it on both occasions.

Angie and Larry held their reception at the Odyssey Athena Ballroom in Los Angeles. There is never a dull moment in a union of two stage performers. After the meal, for their first dance, Angie and Larry took to the floor and began dancing to Ray Charles' iconic song "Come Rain or Come Shine." Suddenly, the music began to skip right in the middle of the song. Angie and Larry paused patiently in each other's arms, as the DJ tried desperately to fix the situation. It was unfortunate as the whole ceremony and reception had been such an elegant, exquisite affair. To make matters worse, the track had now jumped to some sort of tango—not a romantic first dance.

Suddenly, Larry whipped out a rose from his pocket and Angie and Larry began to dance an intricately choreographed tango! The guests began to hoot and holler in delight as it dawned on everyone that the whole thing had been a set-up from the beginning. We later found out that Angie and Larry had been taking dance lessons to prepare for this moment. They hadn't told a soul.

In 1995, Muriel and I took a cruise to Puerto Rico and the Caribbean Islands with our two daughters, their new husbands, and other extended family members. We happened to arrive in Puerto Rico on Good Friday. When we got to the hotel, I rushed out to observe a live Passion Play being performed in the streets of San Juan, and videotaped the re-enactment of Jesus carrying his cross with the soldiers and others.

Leroy and Valerie also came on the trip, as did Stafford's Uncle Merlin (Leroy's brother) and Aunt Jean (his wife). The first night we came down for dinner, we were all hugging and kissing each other, and the steward said, "You folks sure got acquainted quickly." We said we were all one family. He gaped momentarily, then quickly regained his composure; we were such a racially diverse group.

I introduced my wife and two daughters and one son-in-law, Larry, who were all African American. Stafford introduced his parents and his aunt and uncle who were white. Then Larry, being a comedian, completely flummoxed the steward, hugging Stafford's Aunt Jean as he said, "And this is my mother." We all laughed and laughed at the confusion on the steward's face. The rest of the cruise, Larry called Staff's Aunt Jean "Mom" and she called him "Son."

The next evening, after dinner, we all went to the karaoke lounge, and Stafford, who had sung with a boys' choir in his youth, sang a beautiful song that got him loads of applause. Next, Angie, a lifelong professional performer and Tony award winner, took the mic. Her rendition of "My Funny Valentine" blew the audience away; she received a standing ovation.

Not to be outdone, Larry came to the stage and sang "The Candy Man" while impersonating Sammy Davis Jr., complete with hilarious side patter. Larry's performance brought the house down! The whole place was in stitches.

Word of the incredible night of entertainment in the club lounge spread quickly, and the next night, the place was jam-packed. But the manager told the eager attendees that there was no cruise-directed show planned. The performances last night had just been a few talented passengers dropping by the lounge for drinks. For the rest of the cruise, complete strangers would come up to our group and ask if we were planning to go to the club lounge that night. There were so many fun things to do on the ship, we never did make it back to the club lounge for more karaoke.

That week on our Caribbean family cruise, we formed many priceless memories. None of us knew it at the time, but Valerie and Leroy would not be with us much longer. Thank God we were able to share that precious time together.

My mother – the life of the party!

My family – L to R, Back – Doris, Robert, Fredia,
Beulah, Front – Aloysius, Mother, Me

Hawaii and Kailua Jones – L to R, Back row: me, Muriel, Elizabeth and
Al, Center row: Jeanette, Jacqueline,
Front row: Leilani, Al Jr., Kim

Me and Aloysius

Angie/Leilani (middle) originating the role of
Chiffon in *Little Shop of Horrors*

Angie/Leilani accepting a Tony Award for
Best Actress in a Musical in Grind in 1985 (above)
and at the Tony Awards ceremony
with Punahou classmate Willie Falk (below)

Kim's wedding in 1993 - L to R: Muriel, me, Kim, Stafford Nelson, Leroy and Valerie Nelson (Stafford's parents)

Angie's wedding in 1994

Al Jr.'s wedding in 2009 L to R: Joe and Eileen Colling (Kathleen's parents), Kathleen, Al, Muriel and me

GRANDPARENTS

Our first grandchild, Angie and Larry's son John, was born in 1996 at Pomona Valley Hospital in Pomona. We gave our next-door neighbor the keys to our house in Hawaii and flew to California for three months to help out with the new baby. John had a difficult birth and had to be put in an incubator. Angie had a very hard labor and was recovering from medical complications. It was heartbreaking that she could not go to see John and John could not be brought to her.

Muriel and I put on special gowns and gloves to visit John.

When Muriel first saw John, she said, "The baby is under stress! Give him to me!"

The doctor said, "Give her the baby! She knows what she is doing and we can use the extra set of hands." He knew Muriel would provide the baby with love and care and was happy to have her help out.

Muriel wouldn't let me hold John but for five minutes. I said, "I'm going to spend time with *my* baby, Angie." I reassured Angie that Mom was now taking loving care of Baby John and that he would be fine.

We spent many days at the hospital until finally Angie could visit Baby John. We were overjoyed when mother and son could finally go home.

Angie's second child, Lauren, was born in 1998. She had a very fair complexion, blue eyes, and blond hair. The running joke in our family was that Angie had better not give up Lauren to a nurse because she would not get her back; they would never believe she was Lauren's mom!

Back at home, Muriel and I enjoyed giving John and Lauren baths and feeding them. We were sad to return home about a few months after the birth of each of our grandchildren.

Another grandchild joined the family when Kim gave birth to a daughter, Samantha, on April 29, 1999. It had taken her and Stafford six years to conceive their first child. Muriel and I flew in from Hawaii and stayed with Kim and Staff for four months. Kim had limited mobility from her Cesarean section and Sam was a handful as a baby, so she and Staff were grateful to have two extra helping hands.

Sadly, Leroy had passed away in 1997 from colon cancer, and Valerie had been diagnosed with stage IV cancer during the summer of 1998, about when Kim found out she was pregnant. Valerie was very ill, but she was determined to come to the hospital to see the baby. Stafford's brother Graham, brought Valerie to the hospital in a wheelchair. She could not stay long, but it was very special to see her there. Defying her doctor's prognosis, Valerie lived for eight more months, passing away a couple of days after Christmas on December 27, 1999, surrounded by her loving family.

Kim's second daughter, Taylor, was born on August 9, 2001, one month before 9/11. Once again, Muriel and I flew in for a few months to provide some support, knowing that Kim would be having another C-section. We stayed home with Sam, who was now a two-year-old, while Kim and Stafford were in the hospital for Taylor's birth. Sam was beside herself with excitement. She was going to be a big sister! We gave Kim a day to recover after Taylor's birth, and then we brought Sam to the hospital to see them both. We helped Sam crawl into the hospital bed with Kim and positioned her so she could hold Taylor. Sam was literally shaking with excitement. She held her baby sister very gently in her arms and said in a breathless voice full of awe and wonder, "She's so new! I love you, baby." And so, she did. She proved to be a kind, tolerant, and considerate big sister from that first day forward, always eager to play with Taylor and always including her in whatever she was doing. They have always had an unusually close and harmonious sibling relationship.

Taylor was a model baby, very easygoing and no trouble at all to manage. Unlike Sam, you could put Taylor down somewhere and just leave her. She liked to be held, but she didn't *need* to be held. She was equally content to gaze curiously at her new world and play with whatever was within her reach.

When Taylor came home, I noticed that Sam was a little sad because Taylor was getting so much "new baby" attention, so I started bringing Sam a bagel each morning when I returned from daily Mass. Sam would clap her hands with delight as she and I ate our bagels with a glass of milk.

Taylor would look around Grandma's shoulder to see what she was missing. When she was older, we started giving her pieces of our bagels. Taylor could not wait until she was old enough to have her own bagel. As is typical with second siblings, Taylor worshipped Sam and always wanted to do whatever Sam did, oblivious to the fact that Sam was over two years older than her. This would never change.

A NEW BEGINNING

In 1999, Muriel talked me into moving to California. We realized that we were getting older and that we needed to be closer to family; now was the time to move while we still could. We had seen both of Stafford's parents pass away from cancer, in 1997 and 1999, and witnessed how important and helpful it was for them to be surrounded by their three sons who were able to take care of them. And, of course, we were absolutely smitten with our grandchildren and wanted to be a part of their lives.

Given the choice of Minnesota, where Kim lived, and California, where Angie lived, we decided California would be a better fit. We did some scouting around the Pasadena area and found a beautiful new community being built in the foothills of the San Gabriel Mountains called La Vina, ten minutes away from where Angie lived, near the Rose Bowl. The developer had sold all the homes in the first phase of the development and had built three model homes for the second phase. Muriel fell in love with one of the two-bedroom model units. It was beautifully staged and filled with high-end upgrades. The one-level floor plan was ideal, as we wanted a home we could grow old in.

We decided to take the plunge, but would need to move quickly. Most of our cash was tied up in our home in Hawaii, which we were in the process of selling, so my daughter, Angie, loaned us $85,000 for the down payment. We repaid her as soon as our funds were transferred from Hawaii to California, after the close of the sale.

We had lived in Hawaii for forty-three years! Liquidating the contents of our home, putting our house on the market, and making a move to the mainland was a massive undertaking, physically and emotionally. How do you say goodbye to friends you have known for over forty-three years? Muriel and I were deeply woven into the fabric of the island through our years of teaching and my work with the Catholic Church. We had raised our children and spent most of our married lives there. We would miss not only the physical beauty of the place but also the rich racial and cultural tapestry that is so unique to the Hawaiian Islands.

Everything we were planning to bring with us would have to be shipped over to California. One by one, we sold off our possessions. We gave our piano to our next-door neighbors, Jimmy and Linda, who had been so helpful watching over our things as we went back and forth to the mainland and Europe. We sold both cars. We kept things that would help us remember Hawaii and things we could not do without.

I was particularly sad to leave my youth ministry and my Catholic community in Hawaii. Before I left, I visited all of the islands I had ministered as director of Youth Ministry and met with parish youth leaders to let them know I was leaving Hawaii forever. We shared many tears. Bishop Di Lorenzo, the new bishop of Honolulu, gave us a farewell party and presented me with a plaque on which was inscribed, "With Affection, Appreciation and Deep Gratitude for years of Generous Service in Diocesan and Parish Youth Ministry." He informed us that when we visited Honolulu in the future, we had permission to stay at the retreat center free of cost. We looked forward to visiting once a year.

Our Lady of Good Counsel Church gave us a party and a plaque too, dated March 4, 2000, that read: "To Al Jones, in deep appreciation for your faithful and dedicated service." I had been in the ministry there since we arrived in 1957.

Our daughters met us in California. We stored our things from Hawaii and moved in with Angie until our house was ready. By early 2000, we were happily settled into our new home and new life. The furniture we shipped from Hawaii blended very well with the furniture in the model home. Best of all, we were close to our family. We later came to realize what a blessing this move was. Had we waited another ten years, we literally might not have been able to make the move. But more importantly, the timing was significant to us financially. To purchase our new home in California, we had liquidated our stock market investments. Shortly after our purchase, in March of 2001, the dot-com bubble burst, the stock market crashed, and the country fell into recession. We were not impacted because we had invested our resources in our new home. God works in mysterious ways.

Shortly after the move, Sister Kathleen, the director of Religious Education and my old boss, called to invite me to accompany her on one final trip to Samoa for a mission to teach all the youth ministers the latest techniques I had learned at the Los Angeles Catholic Religious Education Congress. All of my expenses would be paid to return to Hawaii for a week to prepare for and take the trip with Sister Kathleen, who would conduct classes for the teachers at parish schools, and with Father Marc Alexander, the Diocesan theologian, who would conduct classes for the priests.

The Samoan Catholic Church asked a prince of the royal family to help me settle in. The king of Samoa gave his permission for us to teach in Samoa Pago Pago and was delighted to have his son be my companion during the visit. I was the first director of Youth Ministry who was not a priest or sister.

The weather was sweltering, and so the prince took me to a store where I could purchase a cloth that men wrapped around their waist called a "lava lava," which was much cooler than pants. The prince picked out three lava lavas for me and started to leave. I asked, "Aren't we going to pay for this?" He said categorically, "The royal family does not pay."

At our first meeting with the group of leaders participating in the parish workshops, I rose to begin my presentation, but before I could, the prince stood and presented me with a war club as a symbol that the king had formally authorized me to speak. I actually had to hold the club up each day before I spoke. A large banquet was thrown for us before we left Samoa. We had special seats near the royal family. Huge platters of food were served first to the royal family, then Sister Kathleen and me, and then to everyone else. The ladies gave us many handmade gifts, including a floor mat. What a great trip! I still have some of the gifts we received.

When I arrived back home, I received a letter from Bishop Weitzel, the bishop of Samoa, thanking me for all that I had done for the young people of the diocese. He wrote, "We are grateful indeed for all the energy and love you put into your work with us. I know you have refused a gratuity, but I do promise my prayers as you travel in the months and years ahead. God bless."

In California, I immediately sought out a new church ministry. I soon found a Sacred Heart Catholic Church located a few blocks from our new home in Altadena. I met the parish priest, Father Jerry, and volunteered for the teen ministry. As had happened with Sister Kathleen, Father Jerry said he had been praying for help with the parish youth ministry for some time! He asked me to form a youth ministry team, which I was delighted to do.

Father introduced me at the 10:30 Mass the next Sunday. I was astonished to learn that the parish teens had never been to the Los Angeles Religious Education Congress Youth Day held in March every year. I had been bringing teens to Youth Day all the way from Hawaii, and it was just a short drive from our parish in California! Addressing the church, I commented on how much I believed our parish teens would enjoy joining the fifteen thousand Catholic teens at the Los Angeles Religious Education Congress Youth Day.

I told the parish I would need a lot of help. I prayed for donations to help pay for the registration and bus rental, for trip chaperones, and for parents to help organize the event. I received overwhelming support. I got the youth engaged to hold car washes to help raise money. Most of the money came from donations from the parishioners. I kept a record of their names and addresses so that the teens could send thank you notes when we returned. I also planned for the teens to thank the parish at each of the Masses the Sunday after the Congress Youth Day.

One day, a little old lady approached me to contribute $2.75 to support the kids. This was clearly a significant contribution for her. I almost cried over her sacrifice. The Youth Day event was fabulous, and the Youth Mass that year was particularly outstanding! They had a Catholic high school girls' dance team performing a liturgical dance, a boy carrying an incense bowl with the smoke flowing out in the air, teens carrying the cross and candles, and archbishops, bishops, priests, and deacons in a long precession of about thirty people!

That Sunday after we returned, the parishioners were particularly generous in the collection. I think parents and parishioners could see that their children were happy and demonstrating a new interest in the church. We resolved to go to the Los Angeles Religious Education Congress Youth Day every year. After attending that first Youth Day event, we started the first Teen Club in Sacred Heart parish. We were on our way.

Shortly thereafter, I was invited to join the newly formed San Gabriel Pastoral Region Board. The Los Angeles Archdiocese has five regions to manage the three hundred parishes. Each region manages sixty parishes. Cardinal Mahoney was the archbishop in charge and managed everything through his bishops heading the five regions. This leadership structure ran very efficiently. I sometimes felt like a fish out of water attending these meetings of bishops, monsignors, priests, sisters, and highly qualified lay leaders, but I was able to hold my own when the conversation was about youth ministry.

Imagine my surprise when I was invited to receive the Catholic Charities Medal. It came with a certificate "that acknowledges with great appreciation Al Jones, whose compassion, initiative, energy and dedication has made a difference to the people of the San Gabriel Pastoral Region. The Board of Directors and the Administration of Catholic Charities salute your achievements and unselfish service." The medal and certificate were presented on April 30, 2001, by his Eminence Cardinal Roger M. Mahoney, archbishop of Los Angeles.

OUR GROWING FAMILY

As we had hoped, moving to California allowed Muriel and me to become an even more integral part of the lives of our children and grandchildren. At the time of the move, January 2000, all three grandchildren were toddlers, and Kim and Stafford visited California often. Leilani's husband's career was exploding, and he and Angie had moved from their first home in Chino Hills to a beautiful, large home in the exclusive Linda Vista neighborhood, right up the street from the Rose Bowl.

There was little I enjoyed more than playing with my grandchildren. One time, Kim, Stafford, and little Sammie were visiting, and Lauren said, "Let's play band." So, we looked around for things to use for instruments. I found the end of a toilet paper roll to be a kind of horn. A large wooden spoon and pot made a great drum. A metal spoon and a plastic bowl made another kind of drum. And a plastic jar with a few peanuts in it made a shaker. We marched around the house and backyard singing, "Doe, a deer, a female deer, ray, a drop of golden sun!" making the noisiest racket you ever wanted to hear! But it was music to us.

Angie and Larry had three swings at the top of the hill in their backyard. I would walk the kids up the steps and help them to get on their swings. There were two regular swings and a smaller plastic bucket swing, which I put Sam in. I was busy going from child to child to keep their swings going and taking video at the same time. Video cameras had become small, portable, and digital by then, and I was always taking pictures and movies. Lauren always wanted me to push her more, and I have a great picture of the three of them swinging, with Lauren waiting impatiently for me to get back to her swing. I framed it and hung it on the wall of our house.

We frequently visited Kim and Stafford in Minnesota, especially for birthdays and holidays when they could not come out to California. Kim had an intense, high-powered job at General Mills, and Stafford was the owner, along with his two older brothers, of a mid-sized business that manufactured trade exhibits under the brand Featherlite Exhibits. Shortly after Taylor was born, Stafford made the decision to stay home to care for the kids. Whenever he had to be out of town, Muriel and I would fly into Minnesota to provide extra support for Kim.

Muriel and I loved visiting our Minnesota grandkids! One day, when Taylor was about five years old, she came downstairs to the basement and asked me to play with her. I was quite comfortable reading my book and watching football on television, but I said, "Sure!"

After a moment or two, Taylor could see that she did not have my full attention, and so she said, "Grandpa, you have to put your book down." I said, "Okay," and put my book down. Still not entirely satisfied, she said, "Grandpa, you have to turn the TV off." So, I did. She then said, "Grandpa, you have to get down on the floor with me." So, I got off of the couch and sat on the floor with her. Now she had my undivided attention.

Taylor then solemnly pulled out one of the many plastic My Little Pony horses she liked to play with and explained all the magical powers of her horse, which looked brand new and had a beautiful long mane and sparkly hooves. She told me that it was very clever, the leader of all of the other horses. It was even able to fly!

Taylor reached into the group of plastic ponies and pulled out an old, raggedy pony with a tangled mane and scuffed coat and handed it to me, saying, "Grandpa, this is your horse."

"Can my horse fly too?!" I asked.

She cried, "No, Grandpa, it can't."

"Why can't I have one of the nice horses that can fly?"

She said firmly, "Grandpa, that is *your* horse!"

She then invented an elaborate, detailed story about the adventures of the horses. At one point, I jumped in, attempting to build on her narrative, but she shut me down immediately, stating with authority, "Grandpa, that's not the way it goes," and continued with her own storyline. I just smiled and went along: I was happy to be playing with her.

As it happened, Taylor's first day of preschool fell on a day when both Kim and Stafford were traveling. Muriel and I were in town providing backup support for the kids. When Muriel and I got to the school with Taylor, there were several children crying because it was their first time away from their parents.

Taylor was squeezing my hand with anxiety. She suddenly looked up at me, eyes as big as saucers, and asked, "Grandpa, am I going to cry?"

"No, you won't. You know I love you, and I will be back to get you in a few hours. Look at all this good stuff they have to play with here! You are going to have a great time!"

I checked her into the classroom, gave her a kiss and a hug, and left.

After I walked out the door, I peeked back around the corner to make sure Taylor was okay and heard her saying to a little boy crying his heart out, "You don't need to cry. Your mother will be back soon. Let's play." He stopped crying and started to play with her. She kept talking about how much fun they were having playing with all those toys. Two other kids also stopped crying and came over to join in. Later that day, when I went back to pick her up, the teacher said Taylor was "seriously vocal" and had a lot to share with the classroom. I thought to myself, *That's our Taylor!*

On one trip, Angie and her kids were visiting Kim and Staff in Minnesota, and so, naturally, Muriel and I came to visit too. Three of our grandchildren were sitting outside the house when Muriel and I arrived. Taylor said, "Grandpa, you are saving us from a fate worse than death!"

I asked, "What's that, honey?"

"Boredom! What are we going to do that's fun, Grandpa?"

I said, "Lauren, walk upstairs and quietly tell John we are leaving and walk back calmly."

"Sam, you tell all the parents that you are going walking with Grandpa. Everyone keep calm because what we are really going to do is go and get some ice cream."

The kids thought we were pulling off a great deception, but their parents knew I was taking them somewhere fun because they remembered me doing the same thing with them when they were little.

On the way to get ice cream, we passed a pet store. I said, "Let's go in and talk to the pets." So, the four of them watched with delight as I growled and barked at the dogs, translating the kids' questions to the dogs and the dogs' responses. People crowded around smiling warmly, perhaps remembering the good times they had with their own grandparents.

John was born with an extraordinary musical gift. Once, when his mother was playing the piano, John walked over and gently moved his mother's hands on the piano keys because she was playing in the wrong key. Angie, a bit startled, realized he was right and thanked him. When no one was looking, John started playing the piano. John did not play with the discordant banging noise typical of a child experiencing a new instrument but made a pleasant harmonious sound as he picked out a tune. I told Angie that he was musically gifted and needed to take piano lessons immediately.

When John was very young, maybe two years old, I noticed he had an incredible sense of syncopation. I would clap a complex rhythm—*clap-clap*, *clap-clap-clap*, *clap-clap*, *clap-clap*, *clap-clap*—and he clapped back the same beat! I clapped the rhythm again (2, 3, 2, 2, 2), and sure enough, John was able to clap it back. I changed the pattern to 2, 2, 1, 3. He matched mine and then took the lead and clapped his own eight rhythms, but to a set of 3, 3, 2, and then he smiled at me. He knew exactly what he was doing.

We had all been noticing that, while gifted in many ways, as John got older he struggled with change and transitions between activities, more than one might expect. He could also get very, very frustrated. And John would sometimes appear not to be listening when asked to do something. Not out of defiance, but simply as if he was focused intently on something else important. It was like he wasn't *there* with you in the moment, but somewhere strange and interesting in his mind.

When John was five years old, he was diagnosed with Asperger's Syndrome, and suddenly, everything became clear: how he could be so brilliant in some ways and yet struggle with simple tasks like homework or chores.

Angie sprang into action to provide the support that John needed to navigate an educational system not designed for him and to develop his amazing gifts and talents. She scheduled him into sessions that helped him better navigate social settings. She hired an amazing piano instructor who quickly realized that while John could not deal with something as structured as practicing scales, he could hear music—anywhere—and simply play it on a piano. John had what is known as perfect pitch, an extraordinary gift. His piano instructor worked *with* John. He let John pick the piece that he wanted to work on, generally something he had heard somewhere, and helped him with the piece. He allowed piano lessons to be fun and creative problem-solving sessions instead of boring, rigid "classes."

Angie and Larry soon moved their young family from Linda Vista to San Marino, where the public school system was known for its strong support for kids with learning challenges, and when that became untenable, they found an extraordinary school called Bridges Academy for kids who were "twice-gifted." Bridges had specially trained educators who understood that kids like John could learn the same content taught in other schools but that it would need to be taught in non-traditional ways—more student-led and with a greater focus on classroom learning versus homework.

Bridges changed John's life and provided a school dynamic that was about success and achievement versus frustration and disappointment because the school worked *with* the uniqueness of each student and appreciated the extraordinary gifts many of its students had to offer— gifts that even the best-intentioned public school might never discover.

One of John's first experiences at Bridges was Pi Day, held each year on March 14 (i.e., 3.14). John was new to the school, and like any new student was anxious about fitting in. On Pi Day, the students could not only eat pie but also participate in a contest to see who could recite the most digits of Pi. The teacher had given the contestants a computer list with pages of digits of Pi following 3.14. John entered the contest and was the last student to go. John recited 164 digits, beating the school's record of eighty. Who knew? What parent would ever think their child might be capable of such an impossible task? The next year, he recited over three hundred digits!

After Pi Day, we all knew that John would thrive in his new learning environment. When John graduated from Bridges Academy, he was one of the students selected to make a speech to the parents, students, and faculty gathered. Much to everyone's astonishment, he absolutely nailed it—he was funny, insightful, and brilliant. Who knew he could speak publicly like that, when no one had ever seen him do it before? What else was he capable of doing?!

Lauren, meanwhile, was always performing and always the leader. She was a mini-Angie from the very beginning. Even as a four-year-old, we watched as she led games, dances, or songs, directing Sam and Taylor and instructing them in the staging and choreography of their "performances." Taylor was just happy her sister and Lauren would let her play with them since she was younger. The three of them would frequently dress up to sing or dance for us.

Soon Lauren was taking ballet, piano, and voice lessons and starring in school musicals. She also became an accomplished pianist. Lauren starred in the *Wizard of Oz* in 2008 at the San Marino Summer Theater. She was fabulous! She played Dorothy, the little girl who had adventures in the land of Oz. She had memorized not only her lines but those of all the other performers' parts, and she whispered them to other performers when their memory failed them. She was only ten years old! I remember seeing the movie years ago, but I thought Lauren's show was even better. Lauren starred in so many productions, singing, dancing, and acting, over the years, and we attended everything. The apple doesn't fall far from the tree, does it?

While John was blossoming at Bridges Academy and Lauren was performing in every production she could find, our Minnesota grandchildren were deeply involved in athletics. Both Sam and Taylor got started in gymnastics at about the age of three, and Muriel and I often took them to classes at a gym called Mini Hops. They were always tumbling and doing backbends and handstands at home and in the backyard. They were very strong little girls and talented gymnasts; soon they were competing successfully on the Mini Hops club team.

Gymnastics really pushed the girls mentally and physically. They were small but mighty, with little six-pack abs. Both girls cycled in and out of horseback riding, one of Kim's childhood passions, which she had continued off and on in Minnesota. Taylor took up, mastered, and then dropped archery, perhaps inspired by *The Hunger Games'* popular heroine. But they eventually transitioned from gymnastics, which became more and more demanding and all-consuming, to lacrosse, which the girls played throughout high school.

Taylor also picked up soccer along the way. She turned out to be quite an extraordinary athlete. She played lacrosse and soccer at the club level and also for her school, playing with the varsity lacrosse and soccer teams from the eighth grade on. Muriel and I traveled to Minnesota several times a year to see our grandchildren compete in their various sports. In 2010, Kim and Stafford built a lake home in Wisconsin, and we would often visit during the week of the Fourth of July, which Kim typically took off for vacation. Our family was almost always all together for Christmas—in either Minnesota or in California—and we never missed Sam or Taylor's birthdays, in April and August, respectively.

Every other year, Angie and Kim's families would vacation together in Disney World in Orlando, Florida, where they both had purchased Disney timeshares. Naturally, we would join them! What a wonderful time we had, visiting all the parks, taking the children on rides, and watching fireworks and musical performances. The kids were awestruck when characters like Mickey Mouse would come by our table to greet them at lunch or when the Disney princesses would sign their autograph books. Disney was a magical place for our grandchildren in those years and that made it magical for us.

Muriel and I celebrated our fiftieth anniversary on April 15, 2006, in Hawaii. Although we had been living in California for six years, we both knew we were returning to the home of our hearts, where our most treasured memories had unfolded. We had arrived in the islands in our twenties, searching for a place where we could build a life as free from racial prejudice, as possible. The experience was everything we had hoped for. It was gratifying as parents to raise our children in Hawaii's inclusive, multicultural environment where they were able to develop their potential unfettered by artificial societal constraints.

My daughters and Al Jr. made most of the arrangements for the anniversary celebration. My brother, Aloysius, flew in from Germany for the event. Muriel's sister, Jeffery, and her brother, Otho, flew in from Texas. The kids were somehow able to invite all of our friends from

Hawaii—they were all there. We had sorely missed our friends, and it was a joyful reunion.

A buffet was arranged at the beautiful Hale Koa Military Hotel party dining room. The room was decorated with a massive ice sculpture of the number "50," and a stunning arrangement of flowers graced each table. As our guests arrived, they gave us flower leis and hugs. At one point, I saw my twin brother with nearly as many leis as I was wearing. We still looked awfully similar and suspected many of our friends thought they were giving the leis to me!

There was a program that included a hula dance performed by Evelyn Young, the first friend we made all those years ago when we first arrived in Hawaii. Another old friend, Monsignor Terrance Watanabe, led Muriel and me in renewing our vows. Other important figures from our past shared remarks about our friendship over the years. Our grandson, John, played the piano, and our three granddaughters, Lauren, Sam, and Taylor, sang a few songs for the assembled guests. Our three children, my brother, and Jeffrey also gave remarks. It was a spectacular affair!

Angie and Larry had rented a large suite in the Hilton Hawaiian Village, which is right next to the Hale Koa. After the party, the celebration shifted over to their place, with just family and our closest friends. We hung out, played cards, and continued to celebrate deep into the night.

The next morning, I took the kids to the beach, looking for puka shells. Puka means "hole" in Hawaiian. We were looking for white shells with a hole in the center made by the surf and sand. I bought puka shell necklaces for the four grandkids and myself, thus initiating them into the "Keiki Puka Shell Club" (a club I made up). I made up a few clever Hawaiian phrases and ceremoniously put the necklaces around their necks. I was wearing my necklace too. They wore their necklaces every day after that. I still have mine.

A GRIEVOUS LOSS

In 1958, when Muriel and I had our second child, Al Jr., Muriel's sister, Jeffrey, gave birth to her first child, Irvin. She had a little girl a few years later, Sewah, and we were able to bring our families together from time to time. We all wanted to make sure the cousins grew up knowing one another. One summer Jeffrey sent her kids out to stay with us on an extended visit to Hawaii. Our kids had so much fun playing with their cousins, going to the beach and just getting to know them better.

When Irvin grew up, he joined the US Marine Corps. He was a smart young man and did well. He married, had two children of his own, and seemed to be prospering. But somewhere along the way, Irvin's life took a sad and unexpected turn. He was introduced to drugs while in the military and it completely derailed him.

In the late 1990s, unbeknownst to Muriel, Irvin came to live in Hawaii. Jeffrey called Muriel one day to ask if we could help her try to locate him. I was surprised Irvin was in Hawaii and had not contacted us. Jeffrey explained that he had become addicted to drugs. I told her I would find him.

She asked, "How in the world are you going to find him?"

I told her, "I know where to look." The previous year, I had taken a state-sponsored course on drug rehabilitation to build my skills as director of Youth Ministry. Through this process, I had become familiar with the drug scene in Hawaii and had lectured throughout the state on youth and adult drug prevention and intervention.

I drove to the seediest part of Waikiki where the drug-addicted typically hung out, wondering if I would be able to find Irvin.

Suddenly, I saw him, lying on the grassy area with a few other men. It had been a long shot that I would be able to locate him, but there he was before me.

I shouted, "Irvin!" and he immediately took off running.

I chased him down and yelled, "Irvin! Stop! It's Uncle Al."

Finally, he stopped, surprised to see me.

I said, "Irvin, your mother is worried about you." Reluctantly, Irvin got into my car. He was in rough shape. I knew I couldn't take him home to see Muriel looking the way he did. He was unshaven, in desperate need of a shower, and wearing filthy clothes. I took him to buy new clothes and to a nearby beach shower to get cleaned up. I then took him to get a shave and a haircut.

Once he was cleaned up, I took Irvin home to Muriel, his aunt, and she cried when she saw him looking so emaciated. I had Irvin call his mother, Jeffrey, to let her know he was okay. She decided on the spot to come to Hawaii to visit us and see her son and arrived within forty-eight hours.

Since Irvin was a veteran through his service with the Marines, I took him to the veterans' hospital for a checkup.

They gave him some medication and scheduled him for a drug rehabilitation program. When Irvin's mother arrived, she cried at how gaunt and unhealthy he looked. He stayed off drugs while Jeffrey was there, but when she returned to Texas, he disappeared again.

The following year, Jeffery called to say that she had been contacted and told that Irvin was in the Hawaii state prison for stealing. She knew I was a trained counselor and asked me if I could counsel him. I asked her to send me a letter formally requesting that I do so, so I could obtain access to Irvin.

I took the letter to the prison and got permission to counsel Irvin. It was the first time I had been in a prison. I put on a brave face as I passed through the prison gates. The guards were very nice. They briefed me that Irvin was healthy and free of drugs because he didn't have any money to buy them. He had been moved into a computer desk job because of his computer skills.

I was able to visit Irvin in the courtyard, and we talked about his family back in Texas and what he was going to do once he got out of prison. Irvin's story was so sad and hard because he had been so successful in life and had lost so much. Irvin was educated, had a beautiful wife, two kids, a lovely home, and a boat—a whole life down the drain due to drug addiction.

On one of my visits, Irvin said, "Uncle Al, I'm not sure I'm going to make it out of here." He told me about a fellow inmate who was jealous of his computer job in the prison office.

I wanted to convey to Irvin that this low point in his life presented him with an opportunity to turn the page and start anew. He had overcome grueling physical withdrawal and was clean for the first time in quite a while. I said to Irvin, "With your skills, you should think about how you can use this time to serve your fellow inmates. You could start a GED program to help prisoners complete their high school education. This might make the other prisoners appreciate your help, rather than resent you and might even secure an early release for you."

Irvin took my advice, and as he embarked on this venture, the prisoner who had resented him became his supporter, grateful that Irvin was helping him, and others, to get a better job after release. Irvin's program was highly successful. He became the most popular inmate in prison. His fellow inmates appreciated his interest in helping, and the prison staff appreciated the way Irvin's program had caused a reduction in prison disciplinary problems. Irvin's classes gave those enrolled a more positive and hopeful outlook for their future.

Kim and Stafford happened to be visiting Hawaii that Christmas with their daughter, Sam. When Kim heard that her cousin was in prison, she decided she wanted to see him. I was able to get permission for them to visit Irvin. It was a strange way for them to reconnect, but their friendship reignited and they visited and got caught up on each other's lives.

After the visit, Kim became increasingly concerned about how Irvin would navigate the world when he was released. Kim began to ask herself what she and Stafford could do to help. Slowly a plan began to form. Kim suggested that removing Irvin from Hawaii might help prevent a relapse. She and Staff offered to sponsor Irvin, fly him out to

Minnesota, and have him live with them in their home and work at Stafford's family business until he could get on his feet.

When Kim made this offer to Irvin, he started crying. He was so touched that someone would do so much for him. This was a chance for a new life.

Kim and Stafford made travel arrangements and set him up with a job at Featherlite Exhibits. When Irvin's release date arrived, I picked him up, took him to the airport, and put him on the plane to Minneapolis. True to their word, Kim and Staff made a place for Irvin in their home and lives. They also enrolled him in the Amicus Project, the African American Family Project, and Twin Cities RISE!, programs designed to help with post-prison re-entry and to address any underlying issues that had led to drug addiction in the first place.

Irvin embraced this shot at a new life with gusto and leveraged all of the opportunities before him. After completing the Twin Cities RISE! program, the organization placed him in a job leveraging his computer skills: the Help Desk at the SuperValu grocery chain headquarters. Irvin had always been smart, charming, funny, and capable; he just struggled with drug addiction. It can happen to anyone.

Irvin stayed off of drugs for three years in Minneapolis but ultimately his inner demons drove him back into drug usage. He returned to Phoenix, Arizona in 2005, but he was unable to win the battle with addiction. In 2006, he died of congestive heart failure related to his longtime drug use.

Angie, Kim, Muriel, and I went to Irvin's funeral in Phoenix, which was held in a large, beautiful park. At the funeral, I saw a tall, slender, young man about eighteen years old standing off to the side, and I immediately knew he was Irvin's son. I pulled Irvin's sister, Sewah, aside and said, "Sewah, that must be Irvin's son. He looks exactly like him." Sewah had never met her nephew. She walked over, gave him a big hug, took him by the hand, and brought him over to meet the extended family he had never known. Our family welcomed him with open arms, amazed to see Irvin's face before us again. Irvin's son told us that his grandmother, on his mother's side, had seen Irvin's obituary in the newspaper and had said to him, "You must go to your father's funeral. This will be your only opportunity to meet your father's people. They are your family too." We were so glad he had come.

BOY SCOUTS—ROUND TWO

After my many years as a troop leader for my son, I found myself later in life introducing scouting to my grandson, when Angie asked me to help John in the Boy Scouts. As mentioned earlier, John was very quiet by nature and sometimes shy about mingling with the other boys. I decided to teach him how to play a mathematical puzzle game of disks called the Tower of Hanoi that I knew would make him instantly popular.

At the next Boy Scout meeting, before the meeting started, I pulled out the puzzle and started working on it. The boys crowded around, curious about how the game worked. I gave it to John to explain and demonstrate. Now, John was "in" with the group. He was able to easily explain the puzzle, and anytime the boys had free time, they would go to John to work on the Tower of Hanoi.

I always had a large tent with an extra sleeping bag just in case Larry, John's dad, could get away and camp overnight. One campout, Larry was able to come and spend the day with John and sleep at the camp overnight. John was so happy. He loved his dad very much and was thrilled to have this special time together.

Meanwhile, Angie told me of a problem they were having at her Twilight Girl Scout Camp, which ran for a whole week from noon to twilight each day. It was a very large camp supported by a lot of mothers who volunteered. The problem was they often had to bring along their sons, who didn't want to be around all those girls. The girls' brothers were unhappy and making trouble. Angie asked if I could work something out to keep the ten little boys happy and away from the girls. Naturally, I accepted the challenge.

I went to the Boy Scouts' scoutmaster and told him that I was setting up an Eagle Scout project for young boys at a Girl Scout camp. We identified a boy in the troop who wanted to do the project to complete his requirements for Eagle Scouts. I was his mentor and shared ideas and listened to his plan. He decided to treat the "little buddies", as we called them, like Cub Scouts and have them learn skills that would earn them belt loops, signifying skill mastery.

This young man researched and selected skills the younger boys might want to learn such as shooting marbles, hiking, putting up a tent, putting up the American flag, dominos, pet care, learning about astronomy, and playing football, volleyball, dodgeball, etc. The younger boys could learn one skill a day.

When the younger boys arrived each day, I would have an overhead canopy set up with card tables and chairs with chess sets ready. That would keep them busy until we were ready to start the session for the day. The youth leader said he would get some of his older Boy Scout peers to come and teach the younger boys chess and other skills. The Girl Scout committee approved our project and provided us with extra chairs and tables. I selected a spot that was far enough away from the girls to create a bit of independence, but close enough for the mothers to be able to see their sons from a distance.

The Boy Scouts ran everything. The little buddies were very happy, as were their moms. The buddies camp was going so well that the little boys didn't want to go home the first evening! Some were hiding in the bushes when their moms came to take them home at twilight.

I discovered one buddy, Chris, was very good at playing chess. I made him a "buddy leader" and put him in charge of checking the buddies' chess skills and setting up and putting away the chess sets.

Another boy was always looking for his mother because this was his first time away from her. Chris adopted him. I told Chris to have the little boy serve everyone lemonade at lunch and dinner. That would give him something special to do and a way to interact with the other buddies. He was going to be okay. That Saturday, when the camp was over, the little boy said, "I'll help you again next year, Mr. Jones." On

Saturday, the girls at the Twilight Camp performed a show for the parents. After the show, our camp was over until the following year.

beautiful Piazza Navonna near our hotel. After dinner, we enjoyed gelato for dessert.

Santorini, our first destination, is one of the most beautiful islands in Greece, with its whitewashed houses and blue domes. John and Lauren walked up to the ancient city of Thira, but Muriel and I took the cable lift and met them at the top. We toured the town, visiting shops, churches, and other attractions before returning to the ship for dinner.

Istanbul, Turkey, was another highlight on the trip. We spent two days touring the Hagia Sophia Museum, the four thousand shops of the Grand Bazaar, the Spice Bazaar, and the famous Blue Mosque. The Grand Bazaar is a large enclosed marketplace that is famous for its spices and Turkish carpets. Muriel decided to buy a round carpet. I asked Angie to help get us a good price, and with her haggling skills, she was able to get the price down.

I was walking around the bazaar when a well-dressed guy came up to me and said, "Sir, can I help you spend your money?"

"No," I said. "My wife is in the carpet shop spending our money with no problem at all." He just laughed and walked away.

On July 4th, we sailed to the port of Kusadasi, Turkey, and took a shuttle to the well-preserved ancient city of Ephesus, one of the best examples of ancient Roman architecture, noted for its wide avenues of cobblestones and beautiful buildings. Also within the vicinity were the ruins of St. John's Basilica.

From there, we sailed to Mykonos, Greece. It was nice to just walk around shopping, relaxing, eating ice cream, and admiring the church and cathedral. Most of the churches there were built in the classic Cycladic style, which involves a box base with a sky-blue dome and whitewashed walls.

We then crossed the sea and docked at Salerno, Italy, shuttling to Naples. We took a four-hour tour of Pompeii, the Roman city that was destroyed by the eruption of Mt. Vesuvius 1,900 years ago. The lava and ash covered the bodies of the people killed by the gas emitted by the explosive eruption. We were amazed to see the shapes of people frozen into the positions they were in when the eruption occurred. We walked down the main street and entered the homes and shops, which were also preserved as they were after the eruption. All had been preserved of life in Ephesus up until the moment of devastation.

Our journey concluded in Rome, where we saw St. Peter's and the Vatican. Muriel and I selected the Hotel Sant' Anna, one block from the Vatican, because we had stayed there years ago. They had refurbished it, and every room was updated, bright, and charming.

We created so many priceless memories on our family trip to the Mediterranean; we will be forever grateful to Angie and Larry for inviting us to be a part of this remarkable family experience.

AN UNEXPECTED SETBACK

Shortly after our trip to Turkey, I began to experience the kinds of health complications that the military had been on the lookout for during my annual Agent Orange Health Study physicals over the years. When my illness hit, it hit with a fury. One day, on a normal trip driving to the Los Angeles Air Force Base to pick up some groceries, I suddenly began to have great difficulty breathing. Muriel happened to be driving and immediately took me to the dispensary minutes away. There, my condition was stabilized, and an ambulance rushed me to the Marina del Rey Hospital. Muriel wanted them to take me to Huntington Hospital, closer to our home, but the ambulance technician told her there was no time; he had to rush me to the nearest hospital that was equipped to handle my perilous condition.

At the Marina Del Rey Hospital, as they were dealing with a blood clot in my lungs, my heart stopped. The equipment connected to me automatically started my heart beating again. The doctors had to navigate the razor's edge between thinning my blood to prevent further blood clots and keeping it thick enough to keep my heart going; back and forth it went. They determined that I would need to have a pacemaker installed immediately and began prepping me for that procedure in my weakened state. The risk was compounded by the knowledge that I would have to undergo general anesthesia in order for the doctors to insert the pacemaker.

By this time, I knew I was in serious trouble. For the first time since the crisis began, I truly understood that I might die on the table—that this might actually be my last day on earth. I could feel my life slipping away as a numbing weakness began to spread through my body. I knew I had to prepare Muriel and wanted to say goodbye in case this was the end.

I said, "Muriel, I may not make it. My body is just so weak. I just want you to know how much I love you. Thank you for coming along with me on this wonderful adventure. Tell the kids I'll always love them. I'm going to try my best to make it, but I don't know if I can."

Muriel began to sob uncontrollably as I was rushed away to the operating room. Even as I felt an oppressive weight descend upon me, I tried hard to be positive. As the orderlies wheeled me down the hall, I called out, "Make way, dead man coming," and tried to laugh. I guess my sense of humor was a bit morbid at that point. The strangest thing was that at no point did I fear the act of dying; it was more that I was sad to leave Muriel, the family, and the marvelous life we had created.

In the operating room, as the anesthesiologist was preparing to put me under, I felt compelled to say to him, "You know what? I may not make it. Don't feel bad if I don't. It's not your fault. I'm just so weak right now." Right before I went out, I said a prayer. "Lord, I am in your hands now. If you want me to come home, I am ready. If not, I would like to stay." And in the next second, I was out.

When I woke up in the recovery room, it was dark and quiet and filled with other sleeping, post-operative patients. As I came to consciousness, I raised myself up on my elbows and said loudly, "Damn, I made it!" and the nurse on duty jumped. I apologized, saying, "I am so sorry! I didn't mean to startle you. I'm just so happy to still be here." I asked her to call my family and let them know I had made it through. The first thing I said when I saw the family was, "Can someone get me a ham and cheese sandwich? I'm so hungry." Someone went out and got me a sandwich and snuck it back into the hospital. I am not even sure if I actually ate it.

My recovery was fast. After a few days, I was ready to get up and walk around, and my doctor said, "Great. Hook this patient up with some portable equipment."

The next day, I felt strong enough to leave my room. Father Tui came by my room to bring me communion, and my bed was empty. He thought I may have died, but the nurse told him, "Mr. Jones is playing cards in the lobby with his family." I was ready to go home weeks before they had expected to release me. Today, I still suffer from a weak heart, but if I rest every two hours, I can still enjoy most of what life has to offer at my age.

GOLDEN YEARS

Many retirees find their sixties to be their golden years, but I have found my eighties to fit that description. I have been blessed to continue to travel, enjoy my time with the family, and have fun. Aloysius and I celebrated our eightieth birthday in Florida in 2012. My entire extended family—my brothers and sisters and their families—flew in for the celebration we held at Walt Disney World. My niece, Jackie, made matching birthday/reunion celebration t-shirts, so we looked like a well-organized group. We all went to Walt Disney World together. Angie rented me a wheelchair, and all the cousins took turns pushing me around. When we went to *The Lion King* show, all seventeen members lined up to go in together in the disabled line. The ticket lady asked, "All of you are in one family?"

"Yes, we are!" I said proudly.

We held the actual celebration in a room at the Shades of Green military resort on the Disney campus. The next evening, we all attended a Hawaiian luau at the Disney "Spirit of Aloha" show at the Polynesian Village Resort. The food was not terribly authentic, but it was still fun to see the dancers and hear music that reminded us of home.

I had been to the Holy Land many, many times, but I wanted to make one last trip. My family thought I was crazy when I told them I was planning to travel on a Holy Land pilgrimage with a group from my church; I was eighty-two at the time and sporting a pacemaker in my chest.

Father Vaughn asked me to help promote the trip. I made picture boards of all the wonderful places we would be visiting, and after church on Sundays when everyone was having breakfast in the courtyard, I spoke about how wonderful the trip was going to be. I had visited the Holy Land about fifteen times over the years and could answer most any question. A friend and fellow parishioner, Mary Ann Casas, decided to take her parents on the trip. She was a big help planning prayer services and collecting donations for the upkeep of each site we visited.

My eldest daughter, Angie, was worried about me making the trip, so she decided to come with me. And so, the two of us traveled with a group of sixteen parishioners from Sacred Heart Church to the Holy Land for eleven days, March 17 to 28, 2014, to walk the path that Jesus walked one last time.

Before we left California, Angie and I made a booklet of religious songs and prayers for the trip and made arrangements to have Father Vaughn celebrate Mass with our group at various locations. I am glad she came because I really did need help getting around. I had a plan to take pictures to show to the teen and adult religious education classes when I returned home. My vision was to prepare a "before and after" presentation. I would show a picture of how a particular site would have looked during Jesus' time and what that site looked like today.

When we arrived at the Notre Dame Catholic Hotel in Jerusalem, I told the group, "Those who feel up to it, drop your bags in your room, and we will make our own trip to the Holy Sepulchre, the place where Jesus was laid after he died." I knew the site would be empty because of the late hour—the perfect time to make a private visit and take pictures. If we had waited and gone on the tour the next day, the site would have been jam-packed with people.

I had visited the site of the Holy Sepulchre years earlier during the Easter season and knew the Black Ethiopian Catholics had a church on the second floor. I asked permission of their bishop for our group to visit the site, and he approved my request. After our visit, we looked down from the balcony into the outside courtyard and saw the Greek bishop lighting the candles of a few people, who then lit the candles of others, until hundreds of candles were lit.

The next morning, for our first tour, we visited the Garden of Gethsemane where Jesus prayed and Judas betrayed him. Father Vaughn celebrated Mass at the altar near the rock where Jesus prayed. The site had a caretaker who had everything that Father needed.

We toured the site where Jesus taught the Apostles the Lord's Prayer. This Church of the Pater Noster had the Lord's Prayer printed on plaques in sixty-two different languages.

We also explored Bethlehem, the place where Jesus was born. The site is not in Israel, so our bus had to cross the border into a disputed area of Palestine. Our Jewish guide had to call to let his security office know that he was crossing over into Bethlehem and let them know when he expected to return to Israel. We celebrated Mass at Saint Catherine Catholic Church, which is connected to the Nativity Site underground.

Then we visited Ein Karem, the site where Mary visited her cousin Elizabeth who was six months pregnant with her son John, who would baptize Jesus years later when he was thirty years old. On the walls were printed plaques of Mary's Magnificat prayer of her acceptance of being the Mother of Jesus.

I took some of our group to the "Garden Tomb" in the evening. This site was bought by General Gordon, a British officer who saw this beautiful garden with trees for shade and an old gravesite nearby. He saw the possibility of building a souvenir store and snack bar and installing places where groups of pilgrims could gather and pray together. The Garden Tomb was located about a twenty-minute walk outside of the Holy City. I had visited the site many times to relax and buy souvenirs and I knew our group would enjoy the experience. While there, I visualized a gravesite where a body could be placed on a slab and a large round stone could be rolled in place to seal it.

I had to plan a second trip to this same location, because several people in our group who did not go with us the first time heard how lovely it was and wanted to see it. On the second trip, we heard gunfire coming from the direction of the Holy City! Cautiously, we began walking in the general direction to our hotel. A crowd of people suddenly appeared running toward us, away from the Holy City.

I said, "We can't go that way." I could see our best route to safety was to head toward the Holy City for a block, then turn right and walk for three blocks. We would then be able to approach our hotel from a safer direction. We took off our "tourist" badges and tried to act like local residents returning home. We walked quietly and tried to avoid attracting attention by not speaking English.

We got back to our hotel without incident. At dinner that night, we shared news of our tense walk back to the hotel during the volley of gunfire. My daughter said that her group had actually been in the Holy City when the shooting started. They stayed put until the sounds of gunfire ceased. They saw a woman and her children walking past the Israeli guards who were handcuffing some Palestinians, who had apparently been subdued. No one was hurt in the exchange.

The Palestinians were firing pistols, and the Israelis were firing automatic weapons in the air. It was a one-sided battle, because the Palestinians would have been killed by the automatic weapons. Thankfully, they surrendered before it came to that. My daughter and her group followed the women with the two children past the guards out of the Holy City and back to the hotel. At the hotel, another group heard us talking about the incident and came over to share their experience. They were close to the firing and hit the ground when the shooting began. Some of them got bruises from falling on the rocks. As soon as the gunfire stopped, they got up and walked back to the hotel. We were so relieved that no one was injured, except for a few bruises.

In the days that followed, we saw a stunning exhibition at the Shroud of Turin, featuring lifelike replicas of the Shroud cloth, crucifixion nails, a crown of thorns, and whips on display in glass containers. We also saw a three-dimensional image of Jesus carved out of wood and a reverse image photograph of the Shroud. I told the story of Jesus' passion, death, and burial, pointing to the various items. Father Vaughn asked how I knew so much. I told him I had bought a book on the topic and had done my homework before visiting the exhibition.

In the next days, we toured Capernaum, staying at the beautiful Ma'aden Hotel near the Sea of Galilee. A church with a thick, plastic, transparent floor had been built directly over the site of St. Peter's house. We had made prior arrangements for Father Vaughn to hold Mass for our group at this venue. We used the songbook we had made before the trip and I was honored to do one of the readings. Other pilgrims visiting the site joined our service.

We had lunch in the town of Tabgha, famous for its intricate tile work, where Jesus multiplied the loaves and fishes. We enjoyed a wonderful lunch of fish, fresh bread, and vegetables, and took a relaxing boat ride on the Sea of Galilee, watching a demonstration of ancient fishing the way it was done in biblical times.

Our next stop was Cana, the city where Jesus attended a wedding and turned water into wine. In Nazareth, we had a drink of water from an ancient well. The water was cool and refreshing. This was the same well from which Jesus and his family drew their water; people have been drinking from it for over two thousand years.

The Church of the Annunciation, another highlight, was crowded because it was the Feast Day of the Annunciation, the day we remember the angel Gabriel announced to Mary that she was to be the Mother of Jesus.

In the church, Mary's words of consent to the honor of being the mother of Jesus are printed in sixty-two different languages. There were many paintings of Jesus and Mary in the image of the ethnicity of people in that region. To our surprise, the people in the church were all Arab Catholics! Angie and I met some Arab Catholic girl guides, who were similar to our Girl Scouts. They all spoke English and asked us if we knew Bruno Mars and Katy Perry. We said we didn't. We took pictures and tried to answer their excited questions about America.

We had to say goodbye to our Israeli guide when we crossed the border into Jordan. One of the most interesting sites in Jordan was Mount Nebo, where Moses was granted a view of the Promised Land. I saw a group of Arab high school girls who were visiting the site. Muslims honor Moses in their holy book, the Qur'an, and these young Arab girls were visiting Mount Nebo to honor Moses. I remembered that Abraham's first son was Ismael, whose mother was Hagar, the Egyptian slave of Sarah. Sarah thought she was too old to have a son and talked Abraham into having a son by her slave girl. The Arabs claim to be descendants of Abraham through his son Ismael. Mount Nebo was a sacred site for the Arabs too.

I said "hello" to the Arab high school girls, who said "hello" back. I asked Angie to check with their teacher to see if we were allowed to talk with them. They seemed very friendly. Their teacher said that it would be okay. Their king had gone to school in America and wanted his people to be friendly with Americans and to learn our culture and language. I told Angie to speak to them, and I would take pictures. They asked Angie if she knew Justin Bieber. She told them she did not.

I noticed that some of the teen girls had their hair completely covered, some partially covered, and some not covered at all. They said the king left the covering of their hair up to their parents. In most respects, they acted just like any group of American girls. They spoke very good English. We answered all their questions about America. Angie and I cherish the wonderful experience talking with them.

We rode for hours to visit the ancient city of Petra, which is carved into the sheer rock face of giant red cliffs. This was the site of the climactic scene in *Indiana Jones and the Last Crusade*. It was a long, steep walk down into the site, so I decided, instead, to spend some quiet time having a drink at the beautiful Swiss hotel nearby. In the end, Angie negotiated the rental of a horse-drawn cart and came back to pick me up, and I was able to visit the site after all. We had lunch while gazing at the spectacular view.

We passed the Cave of Machpelah, where we had to have an armed Israeli Jeep escort for protection. We were not allowed to stop at that Palestinian town to buy souvenirs because it was not safe at the time.

At the Dead Sea, we marveled at the place where God destroyed the cities of Sodom and Gomorrah for their sins. That entire area became infertile, but now, over 3,800 years later, the salty, mineral rich river water and muddy banks are considered therapeutic. Tourists come from near and far to float in the water and benefit from its healing properties.

We put on our bathing suits and entered the water. I held on to the fence because, at my age, I didn't think I would be able to stand up in the water after floating. I was right! I leaned back into the water and was able to float, but my daughter had to hold my feet down in the mud so that I could stand up afterward. The mud was slippery, so she had to help me get out of the water. I decided to cover myself with mud, hoping the mud would relieve me of the pain in my legs and back. I looked so funny that one of our fellow travelers took a picture of me all covered with mud. Later, after I washed off the mud in the outside shower, I noticed that after about an hour the pains in my legs and back had subsided. The mud had indeed proven to have a therapeutic benefit—for me, anyway.

After we got home from the trip, Angie and I made a handsome picture book of our visit to the Holy Land. This book has been an invaluable asset for my teen and adult religious education classes. Years later, I am still sharing our trip with my classes as we discuss Jesus' life in the Mass readings throughout the year. I still show the "then and now" pictures of what Holy Land sites looked like in Jesus' time and in present day. Seeing pictures captured by someone you know is the next best thing to going to the Holy Land yourself.

In addition to traveling internationally, Muriel and I have thoroughly enjoyed journeying throughout the US in recent years. In December 2014, we decided to make a trip to New York City to see our parish deacon, Larry Palmer's daughter, Kiki Palmer, in the Broadway musical *Cinderella*. We go to Disney World in Florida each year with my eldest daughter, who has a Disney timeshare, to enjoy the spectacular Christmas decorations and visit my twin brother who lives nearby.

In March 2014, we took forty parish teens to what would be my last Los Angeles Religious Education Congress Youth Day. We started preparing about six months in advance—raising money for the trip, selecting workshops to attend, renting a bus, and doing the paperwork to excuse the teens from school and get parental permission. It was a lot of work, and while I had enjoyed putting the trip together for many years, I was eighty-two and no longer had the energy to make it happen. It was time for me to let this activity go.

Even at eighty-two, I was too sharp for any young person to pull tricks on me. As we boarded the bus and were pulling away, I made a last-minute headcount. My count revealed one passenger too many. A recount confirmed there was definitely an extra teen on the bus. I told the bus driver to pull over, and we found the extra girl. She had arrived early enough to have been a standby, but there hadn't been a cancellation she could take advantage of. We called her parents and had to wait for them to come pick her up. Her parents didn't know she had skipped school to go on the trip without their permission. I told them that if we had not caught her before arriving at the Convention Center, security would have stopped her at the door because no one could gain entrance without the proper registration credentials. Security would have detained the girl and called her parents.

Now in my late eighties, I am still part of the team at Sacred Heart Church that teaches adults who want to become Catholics, and I'm still eager to undertake new ventures. For example, I have thoroughly enjoyed becoming a member of the St. Peter Claver Catholic African American Council, which provides services to the black community. One of the most rewarding experiences I've had in that capacity has been working with black teens, to prepare them to participate in the Martin Luther King Jr. Mass at the Cathedral. This Mass is a special event that brings black music ministry and dance into the Catholic service and is attended by all of the black congregations in the LA area. I was asked to be a lector at the Mass and readily agreed. Strangely, in all of my travels and experiences, this was my first time working exclusively with African American Catholics and with parishes made up of entirely black congregations.

Unexpectedly, a dear, old friend from Hawaii, Father Marc Alexander, happened to attend the MLK Day Mass. He had always wanted to experience an authentic African American Catholic Mass—something he would not have seen in Hawaii, where the African American Catholic community was so small. Father Alexander was astonished and excited to see me as the lector of the Mass, and after the service, we renewed acquaintances. Father Alexander, in town for the Religious Education Congress, invited me to be the guest of honor at a luncheon with the entire Hawaiian delegation the next day.

In February 2015, I received the Keeper of the Flame Award for "dedicated service to the faith community" from Anderson Shaw, who was also director of the African American Center for Evangelization at the Archdiocese. This award was very precious because it was in recognition of my service to our black community in Los Angeles.

Also, in February that year, Kim invited me to join her in speaking at a Father and Daughter Dinner and Dance in Minnesota. I readily accepted. The dance was for fathers in the black community who were trying to become better fathers to their daughters. Many of them had endured—and overcome—crushing challenges in their lives. Some had been in prison.

As Muriel and I flew to Minnesota, and I tried to decide what to say, Kim briefed me on the event and shared her planned remarks. Kim asked me to wear my military dress uniform, with all my medals on display.

The ballroom was filled with fathers and daughters actively working to build their relationships and spend quality time together. Kim and I would both be speaking at the podium in a shared keynote address. Kim went first and gave a speech on the important role fathers play in the lives of their daughters. She said that a father is the first man every girl falls in love with, and how he treats her will forever shape her view of herself and her worth. He will set the standard against which she will judge every man who comes after. Her message was that fatherhood is a sacred duty and that every girl deserves to have a loving father.

I changed a few thoughts in my speech to match some of Kim's inspirational ideas. I spoke about how my life changed when we had our children and about how our children challenged me to be the best version of myself. I told them I had always desired to spend time with my children, to know them and to allow them to know me. I tried hard to listen to them, be present in their lives, and support them in their activities. A daughter has to know that she can always count on her father. I tried to speak from the heart and when I finished, the crowd's applause and the positive feedback I received the rest of that evening, indicated the group liked what I'd said.

In the summer of 2015, we planned a big trip to Hawaii centered around Kim and Angie's Punahou High School reunions. We were a large group that included Muriel and me, Angie and her kids, and Kim, Staff, and their kids, plus Garance, a French teenager who was staying with Kim. My son Al and his wife also decided to join the trip. We rented a large house in the Portlock neighborhood on Oahu right on the ocean—large enough to cook for and entertain our friends in Hawaii. The home was formerly owned by Dolly Parton, the country singer.

We hosted a big party in our large, rental home on the beach for our old friends still living in Hawaii. Even though we had not seen many of them for several years, we just picked up where we left off as if no time had passed at all. We feel so blessed to have these relationships as a common thread in our lives. As we get older, we value the times we have together to reminisce more than ever. The next day, Wayne Harada, the local theater critic, wrote an article about our party. Wayne knew Angie from reviewing her in shows back when she performed in

Hawaii so many years ago. Angie is part of an exclusive club as a Tony Award Winner from Hawaii; when she comes home, it's news!

Muriel, Angie, John, Lauren, and I took a trip to New York City in August 2015, to see Broadway shows and to see Angie's former husband's new comedy late-night show, *The Nightly Show with Larry Wilmore*. We got the VIP treatment, with someone on Larry's staff greeting us, showing us around the studio, and providing snacks in the green room while waiting for the show to start. At the right time, someone escorted us to our front-row seats. The show was terrific. Larry's guests comically discussed the news of the day. After the show, Larry met us, and we had dinner together. It was a great opportunity for John and Lauren to spend some time with their father.

In celebration of Muriel's and my sixtieth wedding anniversary, Angie, Al, and Kim gave Muriel and me tickets for a Nordic cruise in August 2016. They would be joining us, along with my sister Beulah Sutherland and her elderly friend Audrey; Al's wife, Kathleen; and Angie's kids, Lauren and John. The cruise would be making stops in Copenhagen, Denmark; Helsinki, Finland; Tallinn, Estonia; and St. Petersburg, Russia; from August 11 to 20, 2016.

We met at LAX Airport, where we boarded a plane to Paris and then transferred to a flight to Copenhagen, Denmark. The trip was very long. Muriel and I needed the extra convenience of a bed on such a long flight so, once more, we flew business class. The airline provided us with socks, slippers, a blanket, and a pillow. The meals were outstanding!

While in Copenhagen, we toured the National Museum of Denmark, Tivoli Gardens, Amalienborg Palace, and other attractions. On August 13, we boarded the Serenade of the Seas cruise ship and checked into our cabins.

On that first day, we took a tour of the ship and relaxed until dinner. For each meal, we could be seated in the formal dining room, make a reservation at one of the other restaurants on board, or have a casual dinner at the Windjammer Cafe. They had sixty-five activities to choose from each day, including movies shown four times per day, enriching presentations, and music and dancing. We had dinner together and played cards afterwards, every evening.

The next day, the ship's captain announced we would not be able to put into port in Stockholm, Sweden, but to make up for the unexpected change, we would spend two days in St. Petersburg, Russia. We were thrilled as St. Petersburg had been the big draw for us in the first place. We raced down to the office to book the new tours that had opened up for the extra day in St. Petersburg. In addition to a day tour, we secured tickets to see the St. Petersburg ballet, which ended up being the highlight of the entire trip. If the weather hadn't prevented us from putting in at Stockholm, we would not have been able to see a ballet at all. You never know what new possibilities will emerge when a plan changes; it's best to approach such changes with a positive spirit and optimistic outlook.

The next day, the ship shuttle dropped us off at the center of the small city of Tallinn, Estonia. We learned that Tallinn had the highest rate of internet usage in Europe! Toompea Castle was a great site. We were able to hear a concert of classical music in St. Nicholas Church, which was very restful after walking around all day.

Next, it was finally time to see St. Petersburg. We left the ship for our tours and were expedited through Russian customs. We took a narrated, sightseeing drive through the city of St. Petersburg, admiring the beautiful, onion-domed buildings and colorful architecture of the old town.

When we passed through Russian customs on our way back to the ship, I gave my passport to the female officer, Nadia, a nice-looking woman about thirty years old with a pleasant personality. She clearly enjoyed her job. Unfortunately, just as we passed through her station, there was a computer glitch that caused a terrible delay. Nadia apologized and said the delay might last up to an hour. I told her I was in no real hurry. She said she liked my hat (I always travel with a Hawaiian straw hat). I told her it had been made in Hawaii to celebrate our fiftieth anniversary. She said with amazement, "You lived in Hawaii?!" She had never met anyone from Hawaii before, and we had a great time talking about the islands. She dreamed of living in Hawaii—on an island where the weather was always warm, and you can swim every day of the year.

I answered all her questions about the island, assuring her that girls don't walk around in hula skirts or live in grass huts. She laughed about how life wasn't like the movies. I told her my wife and I had decided to leave Hawaii after forty years because our three children had moved to the mainland when they were raising their families. We moved to California where the weather was very good all year and visited Hawaii once a year to see our friends. I shared that we were going to be there in St. Petersburg for two days, and I was looking forward to seeing the ballet the following evening. She was surprised at how much I knew about St. Petersburg. We talked for about thirty minutes. I think the other people in line, many of whom were quite frustrated, must have wondered what in the heck we could be talking about for half an hour, that was so interesting.

When the computer finally came back online, Nadia said she would never forget her conversation with someone who had actually lived in Hawaii. She thanked me for being such a good sport about waiting so long. I said she was a great conversationalist. "What does that mean?" she asked. I told her it meant that I had enjoyed talking to her very much. She laughed and said, "I have to remember that word." I finally boarded the ship and joined my family.

During our second day in St. Petersburg, we toured the Catherine Palace, one of the world's most beautiful palaces, marveling at the Portrait Gallery, the Throne Room, the legendary Amber Room, and other attractions. Catherine the Great married into the Russian royal family in 1745. After her husband ascended to the throne as Peter the Third, Catherine was able to orchestrate a coup to become empress of Russia in 1762. Her husband, Peter, had alienated the nobles and military and angered the Orthodox Church by taking away their lands. They used Catherine to get rid of Peter. After three decades as Russia's absolute ruler, she died in 1796.

That evening, we saw the St. Petersburg Ballet perform Tchaikovsky's *Swan Lake*. At intermission, we had snacks and champagne. The ballet was great, but what really made it special was that after the performance, the soloists came back on stage to answer audience questions (translated by our guide). We had a great opportunity to learn about the life of the dancers. The ballet was the highlight of our trip.

On August 18, we docked in Helsinki, Finland, where we met Annie, a Finnish friend of Angie's who had lived in America for many years. Annie had a warm and enthusiastic personality and was very happy to see friends from California. Her son had been in the Boy Scouts with

John and me. I remember she was a great mother who attended all the scouting events in support of her son. Annie showed us around her city and took us to a spectacular buffet lunch in a beautiful hotel. We spent hours reminiscing about her life in America with her son, who was away at college and hearing about how wonderful it was for her to be back at home in Helsinki. It is always so special to visit a place where you have friends. It makes the visit more personable.

After St. Petersburg, we made our way back to Copenhagen and then made the long journey home.

It had been a busy travel year, but in October Muriel and I decided to join Angie and her friend Donna on a trip to NYC to visit Lauren at Barnard/Columbia University. Muriel's sister Jeffrey flew in from Austin to join us. We stayed at the Phillips Club Hotel as usual and caught a few musicals on Broadway. We also had a chance to entertain, inviting friends over for small dinner parties and playing cards. It was also wonderful to spend some time with Lauren, whom we missed terribly.

A week later, we dashed off to Chicago with Angie, Kim, and Kim's family to see the Broadway musical *Hamilton*. At this point, everyone in the family but Taylor had seen this remarkable production and we were thoroughly obsessed with the show. Muriel, Angie and I, along with John, Lauren and Sammie had the unique privilege of seeing the show about a month after it opened on Broadway and got to meet and take pictures with Lin Man Miranda, who was friends with Angie's husband at the time. Kim and Stafford had made a trip out to see the show a few months later, but at this point, the New York City production was sold out for the foreseeable future. We were eager to see how the production in Chicago would stack up against the original. We all enjoyed it, especially Taylor!

We spent Christmas 2016, at home in Altadena, California, and traveled back to Honolulu, Hawaii for our annual trip to the two-day Punahou Carnival during the first week of February 2017. We had a Hawaiian luau lunch at the school's cafeteria while listening to the school's band play Hawaiian music in the background. As I walked around the cafeteria, someone ran up and gave me a big hug! It happened so fast, I couldn't see who it was.

She said, "Hi, Mr. Jones. I'm happy to see you!"

I was happy to see her too. It was Holli Yamaguchi, a friend of Kim's. We have known Holli since she was about five years old! Holli's family were our neighbors when we lived up in Pacific Palisades, and they coincidentally ended up moving to our same street when we lived in Newton Estates. Kim and Holli both ended up going to Punahou High School and often carpooled. Neither of them imagined in those days that their friendship would last a lifetime.

In June 2017, the family met in Wayzata, Minnesota, to attend Kim's daughter Sammie's graduation from Breck High School. I remembered when Sam was a cute baby who wanted to be moving all the time. We all used to take turns carrying her around throughout the day. Valerie, Stafford's mother, said that Stafford was like that when he was a baby. They had to take turns carrying him around all day too.

I had fun recalling all the activities we enjoyed throughout the years. When Sammie and her sister Taylor were little, they thought Muriel and I lived at the airport because her parents would always say, "Let's go to the airport and pick up Grandpa and Grandma." Now, suddenly, she was a beautiful, poised young lady leaving high school to enter the University of Michigan's Honors program. Imagine that: My granddaughter would be attending my alma mater, walking on the same ground I trod on so many years ago. I found myself thinking about all the adventures awaiting her in the future and hoping that I would be a part of many of them.

In early November of Sammie's freshman year, we joined Kim, Staff, and Taylor for the University of Michigan's Parent and Family Weekend. The university had a great schedule planned for visiting guests, including tours, lectures, performances, brunches, pep rallies, and, of course, a football game at the Big House, the University of Michigan football stadium that seats over one hundred thousand people. It was remarkable to be back at my alma mater.

We had planned to attend the football game, but the weather was rainy, and I realized that sitting out in the rain on a cold night in November in Michigan was probably not a great idea for Muriel and me. Instead, our family made alternate arrangements to have dinner and see a magic show on the upper floor of the Union. We had a great time!

Being back on campus brought back a flood of memories from my time at Michigan with my twin brother, as I recalled all manner of silly things we did, such as the panty raid we made on the girls' dorm back in 1951. The girls didn't mind losing a few panties. They needed a break from studying for exams and enjoyed having a raid led by the athletes. We knew they were going to raid the boys at the Union in retaliation, so we were waiting for them at the elevators. Our spies kept us posted on what they were doing.

When they reached our floor, and the elevator doors opened, we doused them with buckets of water! They finally broke up our fun by sending out the coaches. We saw our coaches coming and ran back to our dorms. We didn't want to be identified. I kept my pair of panties for a year as a souvenir of our first panty raid to let off the stress of studying for our exams.

In December, Angie invited Muriel and me to join her on a trip to Disney World for her annual Disney Vacation Club timeshare owners' meeting. We went to a special Christmas concert with a full orchestra featuring eight trumpets playing on the sides of the open-air theater. The stage had an overhead covering, but we were sitting in open-air seats. There was a teen choir of about two hundred singers wearing gold-colored robes and two adult choirs of about three hundred singers, each in red and green robes. It was a magnificent production.

Later that month, my daughter Kim retired after nearly thirty years with General Mills. She had worked her way up through the marketing organization to become the President of the Snack Food Division before being promoted to Senior Vice President of External Relations and President of the General Mills Foundation, a job on the executive team of General Mills, reporting to the CEO.

Our family received an invitation to attend Kim's retirement celebration from the CEO of General Mills, Jeff Harmening. We all flew in to be there, including my sister Beulah, our daughter Angie and her two children John and Lauren, and our son Al and his wife Kathleen. At the event were business colleagues, friends, family, and community leaders Kim had worked with. Both the current and past CEOs of General Mills gave remarks at the event as did some of the African American employees Kim had mentored over the years. Kim was recognized as a champion and trailblazer over the course of her career with the company. They remembered her as a "velvet hammer" who consistently produced outstanding results while supporting those around her.

It was a white Christmas in Minnesota and we had so much fun being together, opening presents, and going to Mass at the incomparable Father Kevin McDonough's new church, the Immaculate Conception Church.

After Mass, Father Kevin invited us all to the rectory for snacks and drinks. We had known Father Kevin for many years; he had baptized both of Kim's children, and we considered him part of the family. He used to come over to my daughter's home for dinner and cards. Father Kevin is a whiz at bid whist. He once played in a game with Marc Belton, one of Kim's African American mentors at General Mills, who was a brilliant card player too. Those two talked smack the entire game, which was one for the record books. In the end, Father Kevin and his partner won the game.

"I ain't never been beat like that by no white boy before!" Marc joked. We all laughed and laughed that night.

In May 2018, Kim was honored as the inaugural recipient of the YWCA Minneapolis Woman of Power Award for her work in the community. This award is presented to an individual who has shown extraordinary leadership, dedication, and achievement in all of YWCA's core values—peace, justice, freedom, and dignity. Muriel and I flew for the award presentation; we were so proud to see her receive this recognition.

After nearly 20 years with Intel, Al Jr. elected to take an early retirement (I guess early retirements are something of a tradition in our family), and he and his wife decided to move back to Denver where they first met and Kathleen had family nearby. Al, now semi-retired, decided to become a realtor, passed the state exam, and became a licensed broker.

In 2018, the most amazing event occurred: Al and Kathleen had their first child, a healthy, baby boy! This was a particular blessing in our family because they had been trying to have a child for several years, and Al Jr. was fast approaching sixty years of age. Also, my son was the last living male carrying the Jones family name. Now, with the birth of Baby Al, the family name will continue on.

We flew to Denver to meet our newest grandchild a few days after he was born. Angie and Kim flew in too. Al said that at the hospital, they didn't have any trouble bringing him his baby because he looked just like him. I think he looks like both of his parents.

It was amazing having a new baby in the family. I wasn't able to lift up Baby Al because I have arthritis, and he was too heavy, but if someone put him in my lap, I could hold him to my heart's content. Muriel, Angie, and Kim enjoyed picking him up, walking around with him, and playing with him. Al and Kathleen were great parents. Baby Al was easy to manage after you figured out his eating schedule, potty changing routine, playing time, and sleeping time. He was such a happy baby!

Al had given up his career in real estate to take care of Baby Al, so that he and Kathleen would not both be working, but when Baby Al was about one year old, he decided to go back into the workforce part-time as a federal screening officer at the Denver airport, which was close to home.

We traveled with Angie to Disney World in December and had the opportunity to visit my twin brother Al and his family. Newly retired, Kim was able to join us this time. Stafford stayed with Taylor, who was still in high school. This year, my brother's wife, Elizabeth, was able to make the hour-long trip from their home to Disney World, and come visit us at Kidani Village, the Disney timeshare near Animal Kingdom. We put her in a wheelchair and took her to the main lodge, where she enjoyed getting to experience all of the beautiful Christmas decorations and music. The family also enjoyed seeing the giraffes, gazelles, cranes, storks, zebras, and other wildlife visible on the property.

Muriel, Angie, John, Lauren, and I went back to Colorado for Baby Al's baptism in December 2018. He had already grown so much! This was Lauren and John's first time seeing the baby. Baby Al had seven people to play with him and clearly enjoyed the extra attention. He smiled at everyone and tried to make eye contact in the hope that he would be picked up, otherwise, he was perfectly happy playing with his toys. Al said he knew when to feed or change Baby Al by the different sounds he made. His mode of transportation was rolling around instead of crawling. He loved to eat! Al would tap the bowl and he would open his mouth to be fed. We could see how wonderfully Al and Kathleen attended to Baby Al's needs. It is so much fun to be around a new baby who is happy and charming—we had an absolute ball getting to know him.

At the start of 2019, Angie, Kim, Muriel, and I traveled to Hawaii for the Punahou Carnival annual fundraiser. The three of us had been going to carnival together for several years, but it was Kim's first time attending since graduating from high school. We stayed at an Airbnb housed in the beautiful Luana Hotel in Waikiki. The spacious, private apartment was decorated in the style of old Hawaii, with an outrigger canoe hanging from the ceiling. The room also featured a large, comfortably furnished outdoor deck. It was perfect!

Angie's old high school friend, Willy Falk, had booked a nightclub act at the Blue Note Hawaii club in Waikiki. Like Angie, Willy had realized his dream of a successful career on Broadway, and was even nominated for a Tony Award for his performance as a lead in the musical, *Miss Saigon*. Willy had made good his high school promise and invited Angie to be his date at the Tony Awards. What are the odds of two kids from Hawaii making it on Broadway?! After years performing in musical theater in New York, Willy had gone on to become a successful opera singer. Now he was back home for a couple of weeks, performing for local audiences.

Willy invited Angie to sing a few songs with him as a special guest in his nightclub act. The audience was absolutely packed with friends and family from Punahou and people from the local theater community who remembered Angie and Willy from days gone by. We had reserved seats in the front row for opening night and reveled in hearing our daughter perform on stage, once again, and in seeing Willy join her for a few duets. And, of course, Wayne Harada wrote a wonderful review in the newspaper.

Angie's daughter, Lauren, spent her junior year studying abroad: one semester in Harbin, China, followed by another semester in Paris. We all decided to make a trip to Paris for her last week of school. Angie would go on from that visit to meet up with a group of friends in Italy, and Muriel and I would fly back to LA on the same fight with Lauren.

As often happens with our family, others soon joined the party! Muriel's sister Jeffrey decided to come, as did Angie's best friend, Donna. Kim told us that she, unfortunately, could not make it.

Angie told us she had found us a large three-bedroom Airbnb (two apartments joined together) in the 2nd arrondissement, a fabulous neighborhood a short walk from the Forum Les Halles shopping complex and the stunning Church of St. Eustache.

Muriel and I decided to fly business class because the flight from LA was so long, and we knew we would need seats that would allow us to rest. A limo picked us up at home early in the morning and took us to LAX for the long flight to Paris. They got wheelchair service for me because, at eighty-seven years old, I walked too slow. We also discovered that the wheelchair attendant was able to expedite getting our passports checked—one of the perks of my reduced mobility. This was great service! We checked in early and were the first to board the plane—Muriel tagging along as my travel companion.

When we arrived at the Airbnb, Angie's friend Donna, who had arrived before us, greeted us at the door and gave us a tour of the suite. I was walking through the apartment and suddenly I heard Muriel scream! Then I heard Kim's voice! She had surprised us by arriving early and waiting for us in the back bedroom. She had been able to make the trip, after all. We laughed and laughed.

On Sunday, we went to Mass at The Church of St. Eustache, taking pictures of the beautiful cathedral and listening to the organ music after the service. Having Donna along on the trip was a gift. She loved to cook, and every evening she cooked an authentic French dish, such as Boeuf Bourguignon or Cassoulet, in large enough quantities that we could enjoy the leftovers for lunch the next day. She saved us an enormous amount of money, and we ate like kings!

Angie's birthday occurred during the trip, and Muriel and I gifted her a birthday dinner cruise down the Seine River on May 13. The cruise got off to a rocky start. The guests all arrived at the point of embarkation on the Seine, the boat before us, but the gateway to the entrance of the boat was locked, and none of the staff had the combination! I suggested they pull the pins holding the hinges and remove the gate, but that proved to be unnecessary, and after a bit of back and forth, they finally got the gate opened, and we boarded the boat. They seated us at the front of the boat, and we nearly had a 180-degree view. The dinner was delicious! Muriel and I were reminded of the river tour we had taken one night in Paris many years ago.

When we arrived home after the cruise that evening, we had a surprise birthday party for Angie. When she came into the dining room, we presented a birthday cake with candles and sang, "Happy Birthday." Then we played cards until everyone got sleepy.

On May 14, I stayed home to work on my memoir while everyone went sightseeing. That evening, two old friends of Angie's, Connie and Jim Malone, who were living in Paris for a few months, came over for dinner. Donna had prepared another spectacular French dinner. Connie's older sister, now deceased, had been a famous singer in Paris many, many years ago. Connie and Jim stayed in her sister's beautiful apartment several months a year, spending time enjoying their friends.

As we were talking about black entertainers in Paris, I said, "Speaking of black..."

"I can't wait for what Al is going to say next!" Connie interrupted.

"Where did all the black people in Paris come from? The last time I was in Paris, there weren't this many," I said.

Everyone laughed and said it was true; the presence of blacks had markedly increased in the city. While we were visiting, we had the opportunity to see an outstanding exhibit at the Musee D'Orsay called *Black Models: From Gericault to Matisse*, which explored the depiction of blacks in French art over time.

We also attended a production at the Marigny Theatre of *Guys and Dolls*. My granddaughter Lauren had met one of the leads in the show, by chance, helping her with her luggage at a Parisian train station, a few weeks prior. They had gotten to talking, and the woman invited her to come and see the show. The show was in English with French subtitles.

After the show, we got a chance to meet Lauren's friend. In the show, she had a nasal voice that sounded like she was holding her nose while speaking. When we met her in person, she spoke normally. We asked her what had happened to her nasal voice. She said she had learned to speak that way for the role.

The morning before we left, we had planned a trip to Disneyland in Paris. The weather was gloomy with a good chance of rain, so I decided not to go. I could work on my book. When I first decided to make the trip to Paris, I resolved that I was okay with not going on all the outings and just selecting tours and experiences that didn't have a lot of walking or occurred during the best weather. At my age, I can still have a great time traveling, but I need to be judicious about what I do. However, I am always ready for the next adventure!

Our grandson John is now in his mid-twenties, attending film school. He is an accomplished musician, a skillful writer, an impactful speaker, but most of all, a loving and kind person. Before Covid-19 intruded upon our lives, John came over to the house every Sunday to have brunch with Muriel and me. John always cooked the eggs. After brunch, we played cards, and then John would leave to do homework and let his dog, Buster, out. John is full of surprises, and I couldn't ask for a better grandson.

We have also always been so proud of our granddaughter Lauren. We enjoyed watching her growth in Girl Scouts over the years. At the yearly Girl Scout Twilight Camp at San Marino, we watched her grow from a participant to a leader, choreographing performances and organizing activities. Her Girl Scout sash was full of merit badges! In June 2015, as a senior in high school, Lauren earned the Girl Scouts' highest level of recognition, the Gold Award. This is the equivalent of making Eagle Scout for boys. For her Gold Award project, Lauren created an updated version of the *Schoolhouse Rock!* cartoon series, using popular music from contemporary artists to bring the academic content to life. Then Lauren toured local schools in California and performed her work.

Lauren also starred in Pasadena Civic Ballet's production of *Snow White* as the Evil Witch, which the whole family attended. She graduated from Polytechnic High School on June 15, 2016 to attend Barnard College at Columbia University in New York. We flew to New York to see many of Lauren's performances on campus and were so proud when she graduated last spring. Lauren reminds us so very much of Angie. She has an extraordinary gift for languages and has mastered Spanish, French, and Chinese. She even studied Arabic at one point. Lauren is also a gifted musician, singer, dancer, choreographer, and actress! She is currently getting a graduate degree at the Middlebury Institute of International Studies at Monterey. Lauren is an amazing young woman and I can't wait to see what other adventures and achievements are in her future.

Sammie is a senior now at the University of Michigan, studying International Relations with a minor in business, and Taylor is a freshman at Princeton University. I am so proud of all they have accomplished in their short lives, but most of all I am proud of the kind and thoughtful young women they have become. I look forward to seeing how they chose to make their marks on the world.

Muriel and I can scarcely believe how blessed we are to have such kind, intelligent, and accomplished grandchildren. They have grown up too quickly! We love them so dearly.

This year, in the midst of the horror of the Covid-19 global pandemic, we were blessed with one last grandchild. Al Jr.'s wife, Kathleen, gave birth to little a little girl they named Leilani after my oldest daughter. What a delight to welcome a brand, new soul into the family to hold and love. We haven't been able to travel to see baby Lei in person, with the pandemic raging, but we have seen her online and have heard she is an incredibly mellow, happy, healthy baby. We can't wait to get to know baby Lei and we plan to travel to Denver to see her just as soon as it is safe to do so.

Muriel and I with our first three grandchildren,
Samantha, John and Lauren at our home in Altadena, CA

Taylor, Lauren, Sammie and John

My mother's 100th birthday celebration
in Washington DC

Our 50th Wedding Anniversary in Hawaii in 2006

Family at our 50th Anniversary celebration in 2006
L to R: Back: Larry Wilmore, Angie, Muriel,
me, Kim, Stafford, Taylor, Al Jr.
Front: John, Lauren Sam

Mediterranean cruise in 2011

My brother and I celebrating our 80th Birthday with the extended family at Disneyworld in Orlando in 2012

With Angie on my last trip to
the Holy Land in 2014

Jerusalem, Israel

At the Church of the Holy
Sepulchre, Jerusalem, Israel

An extended Jones family reunion in 2015

Three generations of Al's: Me, Al Jr. and baby Al

Muriel, Angie, Al Jr. and I playing bid whist
at Al Jr.'s home in Colorado

Working with the boys at Twilight Camp

Our family after Mass at our beloved parish,
Our Lady of Good Counsel, on a visit to Hawaii

Kim, Muriel, me and Angie at Our Lady of
Good Council Church, Hawaii 2019

Muriel, Kim and I at the Hale Koa hotel
Brunch, Hawaii 2019

Out of a year of sadness, a ray of hope –
Al Jr.'s second child, Leilani Marie,
born September 30, 2020

Muriel and I relaxing in our backyard
in Pasadena under Covid-19 lockdown in 2020

REFLECTIONS

I am sometimes surprised to realize I am now eighty-nine years of age. The years have gone so quickly and have been filled with so many incredible adventures. I can hardly believe all that has happened in this wonderful life I have been gifted.

Covid-19 has disrupted my life, as it has everyone else's, but I have adapted as I have always done with life's challenges, and tried to focus on all that I have to be grateful for, not the least of which is sheltering in place with the love of my life, Muriel. Life is different and my routines are different. I usually wake up at 4 a.m. Each morning, I check and see if everything is in order around the house, sometimes cleaning any dishes left in the sink. I usually go for a walk in our neighborhood to get some exercise, saying hello to any neighbors I meet along the way. Then I have breakfast, get dressed, and attend virtual Mass. I check my daily "to-do" list and catch up on my emails and usually take a nap around noon.

I enjoy the sunrise, the crisp morning air, and the birds singing, and I appreciate how great life is. I thank the Lord for the gift to hear, smell, see, and enjoy his creation throughout the day. I sometimes listen to classical music on the radio or sing a song that comes to mind. I will often join Muriel in the spa in our backyard, where I am always aware of the different sights, sounds, and smells of the day. At midday, the sultry air is stirred by a refreshing light breeze, and the birds seem to be napping in the shade of the trees. In the evening, I can't wait to see the blue, yellow, and orange of the sunset that fills the sky like a masterpiece of riotous color.

I particularly enjoy the refreshing scents after a soaking rain. The plants appear alive and animated, cleansed of the dust, smog, and heat. The flowers parade their beautiful colors and lush blossoms after the shower. I offer a prayer of thanks to God who has blessed me with the gift of enjoying all these sights of his beautiful creation daily.

At night, the sky is filled with stars that form patterns of constellations that are old, dear friends of my youth and of my life as a Master Navigator. I can remember only a few of the fifty star patterns I once knew, but I have all the old star charts, which I can take out and review.

When I am meditating, so many songs flow softly through my mind, reminding me of cherished memories with Muriel and our children, grandchildren, and friends. Problems that invade my serenity are dealt with lovingly and quickly. None of them are consequential. I allow myself an hour to watch the news on television with Muriel and then quietly retreat to another room to work on my laptop or watch a musical or old black and white film on TCM. In the evening, Muriel and I play Scrabble or cards together. I try to turn in about 8 p.m.

I have enjoyed traveling through these pages of time and reminiscing about my life and that of family, friends, and acquaintances along the way. I read these pages often to celebrate the best times of my life and revisit exciting adventures, long forgotten, but now recaptured here forever. I know so many stories are missing, but these are the best parts I can remember.

As I reflect on what has mattered most in this long life, it has been my faith in God, which has kept me grounded and centered; my wife, who has given me three wonderful children and whose love has sustained me; and a passion for serving others, primarily through teaching. These inspirations have remained strong in my life to this very day.

My story is not over; it is still being written! I am slowing down, but continue relish every day. In the year before Covid-19 shut the world down, I traveled to Hawaii, Minnesota (twice), Florida, Las Vegas, Denver (twice), Dallas, Paris, and New York to visit family, explore the world, and experience all that I am still able to. I hope to continue my travel adventures once it is safe to do so, again. Every day is an opportunity to have a positive impact on someone's life. Every day brings the prospect of sharing God's love. Every day presents an occasion to laugh with and love the people that matter most in our lives. I do not intend to waste these opportunities, and I hope to pursue them for many years to come.

CPSIA information can be obtained
at www.ICGtesting.com
Printed in the USA
BVHW081337010721
610980BV00005B/196